BATTLES AND ENCHANTMENTS

RETOLD FROM EARLY GAELIC LITERATURE

Battles and Enchantments

Retold From Early Gaelic Literature

By
Norreys Jephson O'Conor

BOOKS FOR LIBRARIES PRESS
FREEPORT, NEW YORK

First Published 1922
Reprinted 1970

STANDARD BOOK NUMBER:
8369-5435-1

LIBRARY OF CONGRESS CATALOG CARD NUMBER:
71-124247

PRINTED IN THE UNITED STATES OF AMERICA

TO
MOIRA

He told them stories, sang them magic songs
    Of lovers old and chivalrous romances,
Till every thought of haunting modern wrongs
    Was trodden out by vague and fairy chances.
He gave them all the witchery that belongs
    To laughter's bright dominion and to fancy's.
               GAMALIEL BRADFORD: *A Prophet of Joy.*

FOREWORD

HE aim of this book is to retell that part of the myth-history of early Ireland which deals with the Tuatha De Dannan, or Fairies. The author has tried to preserve the temper of old Irish writing in both thought and form, to retain as much of the original beauty of phrase and imagery as is consistent with coherent narrative. To this end, while avoiding arbitrary changes, he has, nevertheless, used sources freely. Though he has relied upon the work of Celtic scholars, notably the finely cadenced translation by the late Professor Whitley Stokes of "The Second Battle of Moytura" (*Revue Celtique*, XII, 57 ff.), he has also frequently retained constructions in the original Gaelic. For the account of the Milesian invasion, the author is indebted to Professor Macalister and Professor MacNeill's edition of *The Leabhar Gabhala*, the *Recension of Micheál O'Clerigh*, Part I, and to Mr. R. I. Best's translation from d'Arbois de Jubainville, *The Irish Mythological Cycle;* for the story of Ethne, to O'Donovan's edition of *The Annals of the Four Masters*, and for material in the early part of the book, to O'Curry's *The Manuscript Materials of Irish History*.

The frontispiece, based on early Irish decoration, is by Miss Grace Barron, to whom the author makes grateful acknowledgment.

CONTENTS

The decorations were made by Grace A. Barron

BATTLES AND ENCHANTMENTS

The lovely land of Ireland
Arises from the sea;
Cloud-veiled the heather of her hills,
Dark-toned her greenery.

The lovely land of Ireland
Is the Country of the Young;
About the fullness of her age
The green of youth is flung.

Across the hills of Ireland,
Over each starlit plain,
With battered arms of long ago,
Glide figures of the slain.

Down through great branches, stretching
Above a ruined wall
Which sheltered scribes of Clonmacnoise,
The broken moonbeams fall.

In stained, thumbed vellum pages
Are tales of distant years,
And songs that nameless poets sang
Of huntsmen, hounds, and spears.

O lovely land of Ireland,
Be this your gift to men:
Bring back the beauty of the world,
And give us dreams again!

BATTLES
AND ENCHANTMENTS

I

THE LANDING OF THE DEDANNANS

Out of the northern fogs they came,
  The race with golden hair.
Were they gods or men, whose beauty shone
  Like stars in frosty air?

ONG years ago, a great fleet set out from the northern isles of the world. On board the ships were the Tuatha De Dannan, or Dedannans, People of the God Whose Mother Was Dana. They had outgrown their own country and were seeking new lands, leaving behind them their four cities, Falias, Findias, Murias, and Gorias, where they had learned not only the arts of peace and the science of war, but magic, in which "they surpassed the sages of the arts of heathendom." Out of each city they carried a treasure of exceptional virtue. From Falias they took the Stone of Fal, which was used at the crowning of kings and was wont to roar whenever the rightful king sat upon it. This stone is said to have been found later in Scotland, where, as the Stone of Scone, it was borne off to London by Edward I of England, and to this day it forms the seat of the Coronation Chair of the English kings. From the city of Findias the Dedannans took an irresistible sword; from Gorias, a spear so powerful that whoever held it in his hand could not be overthrown; and, out of Murias, a cauldron, known as "the Dagda's, from which no company ever went unthankful."

The Dedannans steered south and landed on the northern coast of Ireland, or Eriu. At that time the country was occupied by a people called Fir Bolg, Men of the Bag, so named from their custom of marching to battle headed by bagpipers. The fisherfolk of the coast did not offer resistance to the Dedannans, who had burned their ships in order that they might never be able to retreat; but when the country folk saw the smoke from the burning vessels, they sent word to the Fir Bolg king, at Tara, that a race of strangers had descended from the clouds.

The king at once sent for one of his most trusted warriors.

"Go thou, O Sreng," he said. "Learn all thou canst of the strangers and of their purpose in coming to Eriu."

Hastily arming himself, the messenger hurried off. When he reached the north, he found that the invaders had marched southwest. Following them, he came upon their encampment on Mag Rein, Level Plain. The Dedannan sentinels reported his approach to their king, who sent one of his most distinguished chieftains to parley with Sreng.

The two men drew near each other cautiously. Fifteen paces apart, they halted, looking over the rims of their shields, each man ready to resist a hostile move, but curious about the other. The Dedannan, like all his people, was tall, with fair hair and blue eyes, and Sreng was short and dark. They were both bareheaded. Their dress and arms were similar: each wore sandals, a kilt, and a short cloak; each had two spears, a sword, and a shield; the spears of the Dedannan were light, sharply pointed, and suitable for casting, while those of the Fir Bolg soldier were heavy, blunt, and more suitable for thrusting. The two men stood admiring each other's strength and suppleness.

At last the Dedannan spoke, and, much to the astonishment of Sreng, in the Gaelic that was the language of the Fir Bolg.

"O Man of Eriu, shall it be peace?" he asked.

"It shall be peace," replied Sreng, lowering his

shield, an example immediately followed by the Dedannan.

"Of what people art thou, O Stranger," continued Sreng, "and how knowest thou the speech of the Fir Bolg?"

"I am of the Dedannan race, from the northern isles of the world," answered the other. Then he told Sreng how the Dedannans had left their four cities, of their treasures, and of the magic which his people had learned. He explained, too, that they and the Fir Bolg had had a common ancestor, Gael, which accounted for their now speaking the same language. Each warrior boasted of the prowess of his own race and of his own clan, not forgetting his personal exploits, until the two men, grown friendly, exchanged spears, for neither had seen javelins like those of the other. Then Sreng recalled his errand.

"Why are ye come hither? To seize our land?"

"My king," answered the Dedannan, "has told me to say to the inhabitants of Eriu that he will divide the country with them. He has no desire for war."

Sreng controlled his anger at the calm proposal of the Dedannan.

"I shall take thy message to King MacErc," he said proudly. "But the Fir Bolg do not give up their land for the asking."

"If it be war, we are ready," haughtily replied the Dedannan.

When Sreng returned to Tara, the High King summoned his council. The spears of the strange chieftain were passed about, and, although the councillors were impressed by these slender weapons, they were not frightened, but resolved to give battle to the invaders; therefore a herald bearing a declaration of war was despatched immediately to the Dedannan camp.

In the meantime, the Dedannans had heard an account of the fierce appearance of Sreng, and had examined the heavy Fir Bolg spears; consequently, when the messenger arrived from Tara, they decided to move to a better position for defense. They chose the Plain of Moytura, which is in the present County Mayo, near the village of Cong, and they pitched camp at the eastern end of the plain. From here they could see easily an army advancing against them, and have time to form in line of battle.

The King of the Fir Bolg, gathering every available fighting man, marched to the Plain of Moytura, entering it at the western end. He arrived too late in the day to offer battle; so he encamped.

The next morning the Dedannan king, Nuada, who wished, if possible, to take possession of the island without fighting, sent Corpre, and other poets of his court, to the King of the Fir Bolg, offering to make peace if the inhabitants of Eriu would give the Dedannans a quarter of the island. MacErc, the Fir Bolg sovereign, refused; his men were eager for conflict, and he hoped completely to crush his enemies.

"If, then, thou wilt not accept our terms of peace, O King," said Corpre, "perchance thou wilt agree that, instead of a general battle, there shall be a combat each day between an equal number of chosen warriors from either army until one side or the other can no longer continue the fighting."

Corpre had been told to make this suggestion, not only because King Nuada counted upon saving the lives of the Dedannans, but because he hoped that MacErc would use the best soldiers of the Fir Bolg on the first day. Nuada would keep his hardiest men in reserve until the veterans of his opponents were weary with fighting; thus, on the second day, his own picked men would have the advantage.

"I will avoid a general battle," agreed the King of the Fir Bolg.

After arranging with MacErc the number of soldiers who were to fight daily, Corpre and his companions returned to King Nuada, who was well pleased with what the envoys had accomplished. The Dedannan sovereign made preparations to begin the battle at once. The Fir Bolg king likewise selected his fighting men, and he chose many of his bravest warriors for the opening conflict, thus completely falling in with the plan of his adversary.

"O Warriors of Eriu," said MacErc, "well do I know that the harvest soon will await you, when ye will wish to lay aside your swords and go into the fields; therefore I have faith that this day ye will crush the enemy, so that afterwards our final victory will be easy. May the blessing of the gods go with you, and may ye prove irresistible!"

This speech was greeted with cheering and with the rattling of spears against shields. At the head of the main body of the Fir Bolg, the picked warriors marched proudly towards the Dedannans. That day the defenders of Eriu would give an account of themselves which would remain forever famous. To meet them came the chosen troops of the Dedannans, leading their army. The opposing ranks halted, and the men who were to fight came on, shouting taunts:

"The Dedannans have the weakness of women!"

"The Fir Bolg have the strength of children!"

The invaders hurled a shower of javelins, but the advancing Fir Bolg were not checked. They rushed on, undaunted, thrusting with their spears. When

these were either lost or hacked to pieces, each man
drew his sword, and the fighting was hand to hand.
Up and down swept the battle, until the Dedannans
were routed and the victors withdrew to their own
end of the plain. From the Fir Bolg camp that evening came the noise of carousing, but there was silence
among the tents of the Dedannans; a few men spoke
in low voices, complaining that King Nuada had allowed them to be overwhelmed. The Dedannan king,
having first summoned his leaders and found that
they approved his strategy, called together his army.

"Soldiers of the Dedannans, I know your discontent. Great is my sadness that ye have not trusted
me. To be sure, that some few of our men have fallen,
but to-day has wearied the bravest of the enemy, and
to-morrow they will fall before your swords like withered grass. I have led you to this land, and our ships
are destroyed; never can we retreat, but never shall
we be overthrown. Strike for your future homes!"

"We have faith, O Nuada!" was the hoarse cry
that rose above the Dedannan camp-fires.

At the eastern extremity of the plain, the Fir Bolg
heard, and wondered that there should be exultation
among the defeated.

Upon the morrow, the second day of the sixth
week of summer, the fighting was fiercer than before,

and the prediction of King Nuada was fulfilled: the
Dedannans gained a hard-won victory. This was repeated the following day.

By this time the King of the Fir Bolg saw his error
in using his best men first. Nearly all his troops had
now been engaged; to-morrow he himself would lead
the remainder in a final effort. The king made a last
appeal to his tired army, but he was heard without
enthusiasm. Hardly a man was unwounded; all
lacked the spirit of victory. Quite different was the
attitude in the Dedannan camp, where King Nuada,
likewise, was preparing to lead his men.

Although the weather on the first three days had
been warm, the sun upon the fourth day was hot, and
there was no breeze. Just after noon, there was a lull
in the desperate struggle; the heat had exhausted the
warriors. Each of the rival kings had performed
brave deeds, but, despite many attempts, they had
not crossed swords. King MacErc rested his shield
upon the ground and stood leaning upon the hilt of
his sword. Sreng, who was acting as captain of the
king's bodyguard, was beside him.

"O Sreng, would I might quench my thirst! Then
should I be able to win the victory."

"Go into the forest, O King! Not far off is a spring
where thou mayst drink. I will lead a new attack

upon the enemy; then thou mayst slip unseen across the open space between our army and the trees."

"My thanks, O Sreng, and my blessing upon thee!"

The captain of the bodyguard once more fell upon the Dedannans, while the king, after choosing five men to accompany him, moved quietly to the flank of the army with the intention of reaching the woods.

Unfortunately for MacErc, King Nuada had stationed two men to watch lest stragglers of the Fir Bolg should try to gain cover. These sentinels saw MacErc and his followers, and sent word to Nuada that a leader, whom they suspected from his rich trappings to be the King of the Fir Bolg, had escaped into the forest.

"Take fifty men and bring him to me, dead or alive," commanded the Dedannan sovereign.

Beside the spring, in a glade far from the clang of swords and the shouting of warriors, MacErc knelt to drink. The only sound was the twitter of a bird which hopped from branch to branch of a great tree. The king's guard dropped their weapons upon the grass and congratulated one another that their departure had been unnoticed by the enemy; but, even as MacErc moistened his lips, there was a sudden crackling of twigs and the whizz of a javelin which pierced the head of the stooping king. His companions, hastily seizing their swords, were too bewildered to offer serious resistance. The Dedannans broke through the undergrowth and rained blows about them. The bodyguard was soon slain, and the victors, with MacErc's head as a trophy, marched joyfully back to the Plain of Moytura.

Meanwhile Sreng, in his impetuous onslaught, had overcome the warriors who were between himself and the leader of the enemy. The king raised his shield to ward off his opponent's attack, but, as he did so, he slipped upon the parched grass, and the sword of Sreng cut off the right hand of Nuada. The Dedannans rushed forward and closed about their ruler, who was carried to the rear. Dismay ran through their ranks, but at that moment men bearing the head of MacErc appeared from the forest. The courage of the invaders revived, while that of the defenders, which had risen swiftly and had centered about Sreng, as suddenly collapsed. Seeing the Fir Bolg demoralized, their new leader led them back to their camp, and the Dedannans made no effort to interfere.

That evening, Sreng, now in full control of the Fir Bolg fortunes, sent word to King Nuada, proposing that there be a final battle the next day between three hundred men of either army. The Fir Bolg commander knew that not many of his soldiers were able to fight, and that even these were downcast because of the loss of their king, but he thought that firmness in the present crisis would win better terms. The desperate plight of the enemy was suspected by Nuada, who was desirous, as ever, of husbanding the strength of his own people; therefore he answered Sreng's proposal with a counter-offer. If the Fir Bolg would surrender their royal palace at Tara, together with the government of the whole island, the Dedannans would allow them to retire to an extensive tract of land bordering the western ocean and there to dwell forever in peace. Sreng and his captains, though realizing that they were vanquished, took counsel. At last, in dejection, they accepted Nuada's conditions, and the Fir Bolg army soon dispersed to their homes, whence each man prepared to move his family and household possessions. With a wailing of bagpipes, the conquered people slowly journeyed to all that was left them of their country, and their retirement was not complete until the end of a year. They dwelt in what was later known as the Province of Connaught, where their descendants, small dark men, may be seen to this day.

The conquerors marched to Tara and made ready

with splendid ceremony to crown their first High
King of Eriu. Unhappily, because of his encounter with Sreng in the Battle of Moytura, Nuada
could not hold this new title, for it was a rigid custom
among the Dedannans that no blemished man might
reign. The famous leech, Diancecht, had tried to restore the king's severed hand, which had been rescued
from the field, but he had failed. Then he had cun-
ningly contrived a hand of silver with movable
joints. By the aid of this, Nuada was able to accomplish the ordinary tasks of daily life, but he could not
use a sword. Hence it was impossible for him to perform the most important duty of a king, that of leading an army in battle. As Nuada of the Silver Hand
he was honored by all the Dedannans, even though
he might no longer reign over them. The council of
nobles, accordingly, was forced to elect a new king,
and they chose a youth named Bres. This young
man was of such striking appearance that old chroni-
clers say he gave his name to every beautiful thing in
Eriu, whether plain or fortress or steed or man or
woman — they were all compared to him; each was
called "a Bres." Nevertheless, the Dedannans were
soon to find that with physical perfection is not always joined nobility of character, and they were destined to regret their choice.

II

THE BIRTH OF BRES

Stronger than wind on a treeless hill
That overlooks the sea,
Than tug of tide or the force of waves,
Shall Love, the Master, be.

NE morning, some twenty years before the
Dedannans left the northern isles, Eri
of the Golden Hair, daughter of one
of their chief nobles, sat alone in a
house which overlooked the ocean. Her
father and her two brothers had gone early
to hunt in the forest, and she was gazing
idly seaward. As she looked, there was a sudden
glint in the distance, and she saw advancing along
the sun-path, borne slowly shoreward by the stream
of the wave, a vessel of silver. When the coracle
came nearer, Eri was able to distinguish a single oc-
cupant, evidently steering the boat towards a sandy
beach not far away.

Since the Dedannans were from early youth taught
to show hospitality to strangers, the girl went to welcome the newcomer, whom she now found to be a
young man of fair appearance, richly dressed. He

wore a saffron kilt, a white linen shirt, and a red man-
tle trimmed with gold and fastened by a golden
brooch in which was set a precious stone. He stood
up, as the bow of his coracle pushed into the sand,
and lifted from the bottom of the boat two smooth-
shafted spears that had points of white bronze. At
his side hung a gold-hilted sword studded with gold
and inlaid with silver.

"Hail, O Maiden! In whose land am I?" courteously asked the stranger.

"In that of the Dedannans, and, if thou comest in
peace, I bid thee welcome in the name of my father,"
answered Eri, impressed by the beauty and the bearing of the dark-browed warrior.

"I am come in peace, and seeking refuge," he said,
stepping ashore.

"Thou shalt have both," replied Eri. "Come with
me to my father's dwelling, where thou mayst find re-
freshment and rest."

After dragging the coracle out of reach of the highest tides, the young man, in company with the
maiden, left the beach. They walked to the house in
silence, each looking narrowly at the other, and with
increasing interest.

When Eri's kinsmen came back from hunting, they
also greeted the stranger in friendly fashion, asking

him his lineage and whence he came. He explained
that he had left his country after a violent quarrel
with his father, a king; therefore he did not wish to
give the name of his native land, lest, if inquiries
were made abroad concerning him, he should be discovered and forced to return. Although his evasive
answers did not entirely satisfy the Dedannan noblemen, they courteously made no further attempt to
question him, and granted him protection. His com-
panionable qualities, especially his skill in the chase,
caused his hosts to overlook the fact that the days of
his sojourn were lengthening into weeks, the weeks
into months; though frequently they wondered who
their guest might be, they respected his reticence, and
none suggested his departure.

During this period, while spring deepened to summer, Eri and the youth were often together in the forest
and by the sea. Gradually, the Dedannans' distrust
lessened, and when, after twelve weeks were almost
gone, the stranger asked if he might marry Eri, her
father consented with scarcely a show of hesitation.

About two months after the marriage, the young
man, who had seemed overjoyed at winning the hand
of the maiden, grew restless and moody. For long
hours he sat rapt in thought, his eyes fixed on the
horizon. Upon hearing his wife's voice, he would

brighten and assure her that nothing of moment troubled him; then, in a little while, he would be sunk again in reverie. One day, when she found him thus, he said:

"O Eri, the time has come for me to return to my own country. These many months I have accepted the hospitality of the Dedannans, but I am a prince in mine own land, and it would be ill done to remain forever among strangers. By now my quarrel with my father will be forgotten, and he will rejoice to see me, for perhaps he has imagined me drowned, or slain by enemies."

Without speaking, Eri burst into tears. He tried to comfort her.

"I shall not forget thee, but I will come with my companions to take thee as a royal bride to my father's court."

Eri ceased weeping.

"Wilt thou not tell me whence thou art come, that I may think of thee in thine own land while thou art gone?" she asked. "Never will I reveal thy secret to any of my kinsfolk."

He reflected before answering.

"I am Elotha, son of Delbaeth, a king of the Fomorians, whose country, also an island, is south of this, close to the island of Eriu."

"O Prince of the Fomorians, I shall await thee."

He took from his finger a gold ring of skilled workmanship and put it upon his wife's hand.

"Take this ring and keep it until I come again. Should it pass from thee, it must be the possession only of one whose finger it will fit."

Thereupon Eri went with Elotha while he told her father and brothers of his intended departure and made ready for his going. Three days later she accompanied him to the beach, where she watched him launch the silver coracle. He held her in his arms, and whispered reassuring words before he stepped aboard. She watched the boat disappear, glittering in the sun-path as it had come.

Eri knew that the Fomorian land was far off, and that it would be a long time before she could have news of Elotha; but she was gladdened in her loneliness by the birth of a son, Bres. However, when months, and finally a year passed, and there was no message from her husband, Eri gave up the hope of hearing from him; he must, she thought, have perished during a storm on his voyage home. She stayed apart from friends and kindred, devoting her love and care to the upbringing of her child. Faithfully she kept the secret of Elotha's nationality. Whenever she could, she sought information about his people. This was difficult to obtain, for the Dedannans had little trade with the Fomorians and never found them well-disposed. At last, however, Eri learned, from merchants who had been shipwrecked on the Fomorian coast, that Elotha had regained his native land. Try as she would, she could ascertain nothing more. To her former grief was added a dignity that verged upon haughtiness, and pride caused her still to keep her secret, save from her father and brothers. Nevertheless, the story that she had made an unfortunate marriage gradually became known to her countrymen, and her sorrow created a sympathetic interest in her son.

The education of the boy was conducted by learned men: the wisest poets taught him traditional tales; the keenest warriors trained him to arms. As Bres grew older, the promise of beauty which he had given as a lad was fulfilled, and this increased his popularity among his elders. Only those of his own age who knew him most intimately hinted that his disposition was not in accord with his appearance; that he was niggardly, jealous, and revengeful.

At the time of the Dedannan expedition to Eriu, Bres was twenty years old. He was given opportunity to distinguish himself in the Battle of Moytura, and, since he had personal courage, he bore himself

well. After the enforced abdication of Nuada, therefore, Bres easily became the center of popular attention, which he took pains to keep turned towards
himself by whatever means were at his command.
However, his election was not unopposed by the more
cautious nobles.

III

THE UNJUST KING

Who is he of the mighty thews
Trenching the royal rath?
Who is he in the speeding boat
Crossing the broad sea-path?

T the time of the coronation of Bres, after a great feast was held at Tara, the Dedannans returned to their homes, satisfied that the best had been done for the kingdom. For some time scant news of the High King spread abroad; though Bres gave his attention not to mastering the duties of the kingship, but to abusing its privileges, spending as little as possible in the entertainment of others, and securing for himself as much revenue as he could, he was subtle enough to avoid creating comment. But an incident soon occurred to show the king's real nature.

Bres did not hesitate to gratify his own pleasure: when his mother gave him a gift of land, he immediately decided to have a new fortified dwelling. This, being a king's dun, was to consist of a mound of earth on which would be a great timber house with many

sleeping-rooms. For protection, there would be two
deep ditches, the earth from these being piled in front
of them to form great ramparts. The rath was to be
one of the strongest and most imposing in Eriu.
The work of digging the trenches and making the
earthworks was assigned to a stalwart champion, the
Dagda. When Bres sent for him and said, "I have appointed thee to trench a new fortress," the warrior
was taken aback. Half dazed, he muttered mechani-
cally, "I shall do as thou desirest, O King!" Not till
a moment afterwards did he realize that he had given
his consent when he should have protested vigor-
ously. A hero of such renown might have been asked
to fight for the king, but should not have been required to do manual labor of this kind. However, he
had pledged his word, and every day for weeks thereafter found him hard at work.

Bres should have requited the Dagda at least by
having him well housed and fed; on the contrary, he
had the champion lodged in a small house wherein
dwelt a cross old man, Cridenbel, who in his youth
had hoped to become a distinguished poet, entitled to
honor almost equal to that accorded kings; but failure had embittered him, and at this time it seemed
his chief endeavor to make as uncomfortable as possible those with whom he came in contact. His treat-

ment of the Dagda was consistent with his character. From the first time that the great warrior sat down to supper, the poet, in the next place at table, watched him greedily. The Dagda, who had been working hard, was, naturally, given more food than the gray-beard, who had passed most of his time hobbling about near the house or sitting on a bench close to the door; even so, the champion's portion was none too generous, yet Cridenbel, leaning towards the warrior, said in a whining voice:

"O Dagda, of thy honor let the three best bits of thy ration be given to me!"

The Dagda was speechless with astonishment, as his anger rose, but, remembering that it was the custom of warriors to avoid quarreling with old men, he acceded to Cridenbel's request.

The success of his impudence so encouraged the crabbed poet, that every night he demanded and received a third of the warrior's food. The inevitable happened: the Dagda grew weak and thin and unable to progress rapidly with trenching Dun Bres. Often he had to stop and rest. As he stood thus, one day, he heard a familiar voice:

"What makes thee look so ill, O Dagda?"

Glancing up, he saw his son, Angus Og, a youth full of good cheer, and, what was then of more importance, good advice.

The Dagda's face brightened, but he answered, "Indeed, I have cause for gloom and illness."

"Tell me the reason for thy misfortune," said Angus, sitting down beside his father.

The Dagda then related his experience with Cridenbel; the twinkling eyes of Angus clouded and the corners of his mouth tightened.

"Verily, thou hast need of help, O Dagda," he answered slowly, knitting his brows.

Suddenly his face cleared, and he sprang to his feet. Plunging his hand into the sporan, or pouch, that hung at the front of his kilt, he drew out three pieces of gold.

"I have solved thy problem," he said. "Take these, and when Cridenbel asks for the three best bits of thy portion, place the gold pieces before him, for, truly, since the king has not yet offered thee payment for thy labor, they are the best bits thou hast received to-day. Perchance Cridenbel will eat them, and, if he does, they will slay him. If thou art seized and brought before Bres, thou wilt be accused of killing Cridenbel by means of a deadly herb. Then thou mayst say, 'What thou utterest, O King of the warriors, is not a prince's truth!' Well must thou, Father, remember the rhyme which describes a good king, a man who knows both mercy and justice and who understands the weaknesses of men:

A good king sits in judgment;
Before his throne are brought
Freemen, slaves, and beggars,
Chieftains who have fought.
Mildly he surveys them,
Speaks a prince's truth:
'Justice knoweth right and wrong;
Here stands neither weak nor strong;
Weak may be in weakness here;
Strong a righteous strength may bear.'

Say these lines to the king, and tell him how thou wert watched by Cridenbel, and how he used to say, 'Give me, O Dagda, the three best bits of thy portion; bad is my housekeeping to-night!' Say to Bres, 'I should have perished of hunger had I not put my best, these three bits of gold, on my ration and given it to Cridenbel; hence the gold is inside Cridenbel and he died of it.' Try, O Dagda, what I suggest, for, if all goes as hitherto, thou wilt surely die."

Warmly thanking his son, the Dagda hurried to his lodging. Everything occurred as had been foretold. Cridenbel, who was half blind, eagerly seized the food upon which were the bars of gold and swallowed them. Writhing in agony, he fell to the floor and died without being able to say what had happened to him.

The Dagda was arrested and taken under guard to Tara, where he was brought into the presence of

Bres, who was sitting in judgment in the great hall. Accused of murdering Cridenbel, the champion defended himself as Angus had counseled him. Bres ordered the body of the dead man opened; the three pieces of gold were discovered, and the prisoner was released.

The trial caused widespread interest among the Dedannans. The Dagda was most popular, and the story of his treatment by the king was told throughout the country, causing general resentment. The High King's subjects had hoped that he would be generous and active in advancing his good name; now they realized that he was anything but the hospitable, kindly monarch they would have respected. Nor did it increase his popularity when it was found that he had been granting a pension to Cridenbel, who was generally disliked. Murmurs against Bres arose on all sides, gathering volume when there became known a second story of his injustice, that of his treatment of Ogma, another famous champion.

Like the Dagda, Ogma had been summoned by Bres and asked to do hard manual work, to bring fuel for the palace at Tara. This champion, too, had been so surprised that he did not protest. He, in his turn, was ill-lodged and ill-fed. Although he was a man of such unusual strength that he carried firewood daily from the distant Clew Bay islands, off the western coast of Eriu, his health began to fail. Once he was so weak when he reached the mainland with his load that he had to stop on the beach for rest, and the tide carried off two thirds of his burden. Arrived at Tara, he was sharply reprimanded by Bres. This was more than Ogma could bear; therefore, telling Bres that he was an ungrateful sovereign, the champion retired to the protection of his own family and clan, and the High King dared not pursue him.

Indignation against the king grew widespread. A greater cause for disquiet was the fact that the Fomorians, from headquarters on Tory Island, close to the northern shore of Eriu, had begun to make raids upon the Dedannans, plundering and wasting the land if they were opposed. These Fomorians were men of huge stature, violent and unscrupulous, no better than pirates. With them the Dedannans, on first coming to Ireland, had vainly sought an alliance, and it was partly because the parentage of Bres was suspected of being half Fomorian, that, as a matter of policy, he had been chosen king. But reliance upon the good offices of Bres with his supposed kinsmen proved ill-founded. His subjects on the northern coast appealed without avail for his assistance. He answered that he had neither the men nor the wealth to help them. The Fomorians, becoming bolder, were at last virtually lords of the raided district. To Bres they sent an embassy, calling upon the whole island of Eriu to pay tribute.

"Now," said the Dedannans, who still trusted him, "our High King will treat this insult as it deserves. The ambassadors will be sent back to Tory Island with a contemptuous defiance, and Eriu will be called to arms."

Little did his people know the temper of the king. Perhaps because of his Fomorian blood, perhaps because he was miserly and knew that a war would be costly, he not only received the messengers with courtesy, but agreed that Eriu should pay the large sum they demanded.

"Ever have I wished that my people should live in peace; better is it to pay with cattle, with gold, and with the fruits of the earth, than with the bodies of men," declared Bres.

The Fomorians, though wondering at such compliance, joyously took their departure. However, through the outlying country they had to hasten in fear of their lives, so angry were the Dedannans when they heard rumors of the tribute — news which spread rapidly from man to man. At almost the same time, another event ended the patience of the nobles.

One of the distinguished Dedannan poets, chief among those sent as heralds to the Fir Bolg before the Battle of Moytura, was Corpre, friend and intimate of Nuada of the Silver Hand. The former king kept a lively interest in the affairs of the kingdom, and he was one of the first to hear the stories about Bres. When Nuada learned of the Fomorian demand, he sent for his friend.

"O Corpre," he said, "greatly am I troubled for the future of Eriu. Bres seems to care little for the honor of this country and to think only of his own welfare. I would know whether what I hear of the High King is true, for, if he is unfit to rule, he must be forced to give up the throne. Because I have been king, I cannot, without bringing upon myself just reproof, travel about Eriu to learn the truth concerning Bres. The reports of him may well be idle talk such as ever surrounds a monarch. But thou mayst journey through the country and, especially, visit Tara, without provoking comment. None other is better able to find the temper of the people and to report Bres truly. Bring back word to me, and, if the king has done ill, I shall see to the summoning of the council of nobles, that he may be tried. Wilt thou undertake this journey for the sake of the land we both love?"

"O Nuada, gladly will I do this because of our friendship, and for the good of Eriu."

Not many days later, Corpre set forth. He went first to the distressed north, next westward, and so south, then up the eastern coast and through the center of the island. Everywhere he found discontent. One evening, after a feast given in honor of the poet — for Corpre was treated with the highest respect by every chieftain whom he visited — a veteran of the Battle of Moytura voiced the general feeling:

"O poet of Eriu, well mayst thou lament thy country! Her honor is forgotten; he who should guide and protect neglects her. The insolence of pirates terrifies a king, and there is not smoke from a roof in Eriu that is not under tribute. My sword frets to be drawn against the Fomorians and this traitor who sits upon our throne."

With these words lingering in his mind, Corpre came the following afternoon to Tara. The guards saw him approaching and sent a message to Bres, who was sitting in the great hall. Ever since the time of the Fomorian embassy, the king had been uneasy, but he was trying to deceive himself with excuses. The messenger found him gazing sullenly into vacancy and had to attract his attention.

"What wouldst thou?" curtly asked Bres.

"O King, a man of distinction comes hither. The guards think he is Corpre, the poet. What honor shall we pay him?"

"I will teach him that an unexpected visit is presumption!" cried Bres, flaring into anger. He leaned forward, grasping the arm of his chair before he continued: "Take him to the house wherein were lodged the servants of the Fomorian envoys, and carry him there the supper of an unruly menial."

The messenger looked his astonishment, but he answered only, "What thou commandest shall be done, O King!" and departed on his errand.

Was Bres mad? It was the custom to show the foremost poets almost as much reverence as that shown to kings; poets even had the right of sitting at the royal table. Bres had given the Fomorian ambassadors the best the palace had to offer; why was he treating a Dedannan with indignity? The man shook his head as he went to escort Corpre to the little hut — for it was scarcely more — into which had been crowded the Fomorian attendants.

Corpre's face fell when he saw where he was lodged, and the servant could not refrain from a word of apology. When Corpre found that his room had but a single window and neither fire nor furniture, that he must sleep on straw laid upon the bare earth, he was amazed. Were there so many guests of high rank that he should be put into quarters like these? He would protest to the king at once, and would probably pass only one night in the hut. But Corpre's wonder was changed to wrath when supper was brought out to him — a jug of water and three little unbuttered cakes on a large dish.

Angrily the poet paced up and down. It was too late and too dark to leave that evening; early in the morning he would be up and away. He would not, as he had planned, pass several days with the High King; he would speed back to Nuada and tell him of the treatment of guests at Tara. Sleeping little, he spent the night in devising a plan to bring justice upon Bres. He would make a poem, a satire, asking that ill should befall the king, and the greatest of the gods would surely answer.

By sunrise, Corpre was ready to start homeward. As he crossed the lis, or enclosure, of Tara, he recited:

"Without food quickly on a dish,
Without a cow's milk whereon a calf grows,
Without a man's abode under the gloom of night,
Without means to pay a company of story-tellers —
Suffering the death of a traitor —
Let that be the condition of Bres."

Then, laughing bitterly, he hastened away. Guards and servants who heard him were startled. They rushed to tell Bres of Corpre's curse. The king's heart sank, but he tried to reassure those who came to warn him.

Within a few weeks' time there appeared on the face of Bres a red blotch, followed soon after by one of white, and then by one of green — he was a blem- ished king, and forthwith his doom would be upon him. Although several leeches tried, none could cure him.

From that day, satires were a weapon of poets in Eriu; but only a just satire was to be feared; an un- just recoiled upon the maker.

IV

THE FLIGHT OF BRES

A shadow moves past the headland, a gleam of wind-tossed spray
From speeding oars; the long boat takes the traitor on his way.

NUADA lost no time in telling of the treatment of Corpre. The council was quickly assembled at Tara, and Bres was called before it. Silence filled the huge high-ceilinged hall as the door opened and the king was ushered in to face the nobles seated upon either hand. One of the eldest of the company rose to make formal complaint against the sovereign.

"O King of Eriu, we, the nobles of thy kingdom, accuse thee of being miserly, inhospitable, mean-spirited, and of caring naught for the honor of thy country — unfit to be our king. Those who have visited thee have found their knives ungreased, and their breaths have not smelt of ale. Our poets, our bards, our harpers, our pipers, our hornblowers, our jugglers, our jesters, have not been present at feasts for our entertainment, neither have our athletes and our champions tried their skill at thy court. The muscles of our strong men have grown weak, and our warriors have forgotten their cunning with weapons. Nor service nor eric, the blood tax, has been continued to the tribes, and the treasures of a tribe have not been delivered by the act of the whole tribe. Hast thou aught to say in thy defense, O Bres?"

The king tried to explain that his endeavor had been to reduce the expenses of government, particularly until the Dedannans should become thoroughly adjusted to conditions in their new country; but his explanations were unsatisfactory. He tried to justify his treatment of the Dagda, of Ogma, and of Corpre, but he was heard in scornful silence. At last, when he attempted to defend his refusal to help the Dedannans in the north against the Fomorian raiders, one of the northern nobles stood up, and, pointing to him, cried:

"O King, I accuse thee of allowing thy countrymen to perish when it was thy duty to protect them, and of being heedless when thy countrywomen were carried off into a strange land."

A murmur of approval greeted this speech, and there were cries of, "Well spoken!" Another noble proposed that the king be asked to leave the hall while a vote was taken as to whether or no he should be deposed. This was agreed to, and Bres was deprived of the kingship. Summoned once more into the hall, he was told of the judgment of the council and was asked if he had anything to say.

"Nobles of Eriu," answered Bres, "well do I know that I have enemies, and they have prevailed. I am content to leave the sovereignty; yet, that the duties of my office may be more easily learned by another, and the affairs of the kingdom left in good order, I would remain at Tara a year longer. Should ye will it so, let men from your council be appointed to oversee my conduct of the state; at the end of a year let them examine anew into the affairs of the kingship."

"Thou hast spoken with reason," said the head of the council, "and we will discuss thine offer."

Once more Bres withdrew, and the nobles, after considerable argument, finally permitted him to remain at Tara for the period of a year. They came to this decision largely because there was hope that a young leech, Miach, would succeed in giving back to Nuada the use of his hand, and there was no other man they would so gladly have to rule over them. The council, however, appointed five of their number to be responsible for the king's discharge of his duties.

Bres was secretly pleased when he was told that the nobles had adopted his suggestion. At the back of his mind lay no really unselfish wish to benefit his successor, but within a year he expected to amass

enough wealth to make himself rich. Then he would
escape to the Fomorian stronghold, where he would
ask aid of the pirates in restoring himself to the
throne.

Therefore, when the assembly was dissolved, he
went to tell his mother of his plans. She lived at Tara
in a house not far from the great hall. He found her
nervously awaiting the outcome of his trial.

Nothing in the world was dearer to Eri than the
welfare of her son; this surpassed even her love of
country. She was blind to the faults of Bres, and unable to see that he inherited the characteristics of his
father rather than those of the Dedannans. The tenderness shown her for years by her countrymen did
not modify her indignation when Bres was called to
give an account of his kingship, and, during his absence in the great hall, she paced the floor, biting her
lower lip, her eyes blazing, her hands clenched.
Keenly she regretted not having told her son he was
not all of the blood of the unappreciative Dedannans.

When the young man entered the room, she flung
herself upon him.

"Tell me, O Son, what has befallen thee? Thou art
still High King of this people?"

"But for a time, O Mother," Bres answered gloom-
ily. Then he told her all that had happened, and of

his determination to flee the country in order to get help from abroad.

"During all the years that we have been together, thou hast said little of my father, save that he was of royal blood. I do not know that he was even of the Dedannan race."

"Truly, my son, thy father was the son of a king. His name was Elotha, and he was no Dedannan, but a Fomorian. Take this ring which he gave me, charging me to part with it neither by sale nor by gift but to the one whose finger could wear it."

So saying, she drew off the ring that Elotha had left with her at parting, and placed it upon Bres's little finger, where it fitted perfectly.

"That is a sign, O Bres. Thou art indeed he for whom the ring was destined. Come, let us plan to go hence into the country of the Fomorians!"

In her son's distress, Eri forgot her sorrow of years, and her proud determination never to approach her husband. Far into the night she and Bres talked; dawn found their plans completed.

A few months later, Bres, making the excuse that he wished to inspect the coast, journeyed northward, accompanied by his mother and a few trusted attendants. Those who met him on the road noticed that he had more luggage than would ordinarily be taken upon a short tour, but only one man was suspicious enough to report what he had seen to the nobles responsible for the king's good behavior. Alarmed, they sent soldiers to discover the real reason for the presence of Bres in the north, and, if necessary, to take him prisoner. They arrived in time to see a ship bearing the king and his mother far out on the bay and bound for Tory Island. The soldiers could only stand helpless on the shore, gazing at the vanishing boat.

   .   .   .   .

The Fomorians were at first inclined to be hostile to Eri and Bres. When, however, it was explained that the Dedannan king was seeking protection and aid against his countrymen, his reception was cordial. The mother and son were escorted to a meadow not far from their landing-place, where the petty king of the district was present at a fair. Men and women from miles about had come to watch, and to take part in, games and athletic contests.

The day was unusually bright; the brilliant colors of kilt and cloak, the flash of spear-heads and swords of white bronze, contrasted with the vivid green of the grass and the blue of the sea. The Fomorian king sat upon a mound of earth and acted as judge in the sports. To him were brought Eri and Bres. When their errand was explained, he received them courteously.

"O King of the Dedannans," he said, "we are about to hold a race. Hast thou, perchance, brought with thee hounds from Eriu? If so, enter them in friendly contest with the dogs of the Fomorians. Later, thou canst tell at length the story of thy coming hither."

"We have hounds," answered Bres.

He made a sign to an attendant, who led out two couples in leash. The dogs were loosed, and all four finished ahead of their rivals.

"Swift are thy hounds, indeed," said the king to Bres. "Hast thou, perchance, horses for a race?"

"We have horses," said Bres.

Two spirited steeds, one black, the other brown, were brought forward and mounted by skilled riders from Bres's following. The horses pranced restlessly before the start; then they sped forward as if they had been stones from a sling. The good fortune of Bres was scarcely less in this race than in the former; the black horse finished first, the brown third, the Fomorian king's own charger taking second place.

"Marvelous are the steeds of the Dedannans!" exclaimed the king. "There is not another horse in this land which can outrun mine. But now we are to turn

from the swiftness of beasts to the skill of men. Ever
have the warriors of our country been eager in feats
of sword and javelin. If thou wouldst win thy kingdom again, well mayst thou rely upon the prowess of
the Fomorians! One of the greatest of our champions,
Bel, stands ready to meet in sword-play the man who
will contend with him. Hast thou such an one with
thee?"

"I myself am that man," said Bres, drawing his
sword and raising it above his head, where the sunlight gleamed upon the blade.

Among those near enough to hear Bres's brave
declaration ran a murmur of approval, increasing to a
roar like the crash of many waves when the Fomorian
king announced that the Dedannan sovereign himself would meet Bel. With the shouting was mingled
the clatter of swords and spears against shields.
Then the people crowded close to watch the final
contest.

The two men took their places and saluted. They
had been provided with special blunt weapons, that
there might be less danger of serious injury to warriors whose full strength would soon be needed in
war. At first, the opponents eyed each other cautiously; then Bel made a savage cut at Bres, who
skillfully parried the blow with his shield. There-

upon, the Fomorian champion seemed resolved to end the struggle quickly, for he made a continued impetuous attack. Bres, however, succeeded in repelling this onslaught either with his sword or with his shield, and but twice did his adversary's weapon graze him. Now and again he took the offensive momentarily; he seemed waiting for the other to tire himself. Most of the bystanders shouted with delight when Bel appeared to be gaining the advantage, though all the Dedannan followers, and even a few of the Fomorians, gave encouragement to Bres. At last, Bel making a mighty thrust which his opponent dodged nimbly, slightly overreached himself, and swayed unsteadily as he tried to keep his footing upon the grass, grown slippery from much trampling. This, apparently, was the opportunity for which Bres had waited, and he plunged forward to the attack. Bel had managed to regain his balance, but he seemed dazed, and it was not long before a sweeping blow from Bres laid his adversary prostrate and momentarily unconscious.

The multitude did not withhold approval of the stranger. Bres turned and knelt before the king to receive the prize, a sword with hilt of gold.

The Fomorian ruler began, "No less wondrous thy skill —" but his voice faltered, and he grew pale.

Those who stood near the throne rushed to his aid. He recovered himself, and, speaking as if bewildered, said:

"That ring which thou wearest —"

He paused again, and looked at Bres with filling eyes.

Eri had been close at hand, watching the Fomorian ruler intently. Now she ran forward, crying, "Elotha, my husband! They did not tell us thy name. Thou art Elotha, and I am Eri!"

The Fomorian king stepped from the mound and clasped Eri in his arms. To the young man, he said, "Thou art my son."

Bres embraced his father. There were explanations between them. Soon the good news spread through the gathering, whereupon there was much rejoicing.

"Come with me, O Eri, and thou, O Bres," said Elotha, at last. "Let us go to my tent, where we may have food and drink, and where ye may both tell your tale."

Gladly mother and son followed him; long was their talk.

Upon seeing Elotha, Eri's love was renewed. Her husband told her that, after his return from the northern isles to his own country, his father, who wished him to marry a princess of the Fomorians, had assured him that Eri was dead, showing him a lock of hair said to have been sent by her kinsmen. Elotha had then married. Shortly afterwards, his wife died, leaving him childless, and he had been unwilling to wed again. He had hoped ever that the news about Eri might be proved false, and that he and she might one day be reunited. Then Eri told Elotha the story of the birth of Bres and of his education and of his election to the kingship.

The Fomorian king thereupon turned to his son; "O Bres, what need has brought thee out of the land where thou ruledst?"

Bres told his father in detail of how he had tried to govern Eriu, and of his attempts at economy by reducing the entertainment of guests at Tara. This policy, he could see, Elotha did not approve, for he knit his brows. Bres concluded with the account of his summoning before the assembly, and of his arrangement with the nobles.

"Men say that nothing has brought me to the loss of my throne save my own injustice and arrogance," he declared. "I stripped the Dedannans of their jewels and treasure, and of their own food. Neither tribute nor eric was taken from them and given to foreigners before this time."

"That is bad," said Elotha. "Better were their

prosperity than their kingship; better were their prayers than their curses. Why hast thou come hither?"

"To whom should a son turn in distress, if not to his father? I have come to seek a champion from thee," answered Bres. "I would take Eriu by force."

"It should not be gained by injustice, if not by justice," continued Elotha reprovingly.

"What counsel hast thou for me, then?" asked Bres, hesitatingly.

Thereupon Elotha changed his attitude. His face cleared, and he laughed a low, malicious laugh.

"Although I do not like all thou hast done, should I not rejoice that chance has given me not only a son, but the occasion of going with the forces of the Fomorians against a race I hate? Thou hast spoken truth," he continued, placing a hand upon the shoulder of Bres, "in saying that a son should turn to his father. I will not desert thee. I will send thee to Balor, grandson of Net, to the king of the isles, sovereign over all the Fomorians, and to Indech, son of De Domnan, asking their aid and their authority for an expedition into Eriu."

Delighted, Bres thanked his father, and together they made plans to raise and equip a mighty host. Not many days later, the banished king left Elotha and journeyed under escort to the palace of Balor; thence to that of Indech. Willingly these monarchs agreed to coöperate with Elotha, and soon the forges were busy from one end of Tory Island to the other, where men were hammering out swords and spearheads. In the forest, some were felling trees; others were making frames for shields, handles for spears, and ribs for ships. The boast of the Fomorians was that there should be a bridge of boats from their land to the shores of Eriu.

V

THE HEALING OF NUADA

Fire, kindle! Smoke, arise!
On his couch the sick man lies.
Sweet the odor of burning herbs;
His heavy rest no pain disturbs.
With fingers deft and potent spell,
The skillful leech shall make him well.

IMMEDIATELY upon hearing of the flight of
Bres, the Dedannans were on the alert; they
expected him to attempt revenge. The nobles
commissioned to oversee the kingship hastened to Tara, where they found Bres had carried off everything of value that was portable.
Bitterly they regretted having trusted him.

While they were still at the palace straightening
out the tangled threads of government, there was
brought them word of unwonted activity among the
Fomorians. No time was lost in sending to Tory
Island men in disguise, who soon returned with news
of the projected expedition on behalf of Bres. Therefore, the entire council of nobles was quickly brought
together to choose a king whose wisdom and valor
should enable his people to make the best possible de-

fense of their country. As the assembly was ready to begin discussion, a messenger dismounted from a horse lathered with foam, and asked to be taken immediately before the head of the council.

"Good are my tidings, rulers of Eriu," the man cried. "Nuada is no longer blemished; Miach, son of Diancecht, has restored the hand cut off at the Battle of Moytura."

There was a burst of cheering: men embraced one another in glee; the noise so startled the birds under the eaves of the great hall that they flew away.

The messenger told the story of Miach's successful cure.

When, after the Battle of Moytura, Diancecht had failed to restore the severed hand of Nuada and had provided him with a silver hand instead, Miach had been a lad, interested in his father's work, but unable to help. However, all who knew Miach were amazed at the quickness of his mind and the ease with which he soon learned the use of herbs and the magic incantations that formed the necessary knowledge of a leech.

One day, when Nuada had worn the silver hand for some years, Miach came to him and said, "O Nuada, I believe I can restore thine own hand. My father is old and he dares not venture as I will. I promise at least to harm thee no further."

"Truly, O Miach," answered Nuada, "I will trust myself to thy care, for I like thy boldness. Of little use is this silver hand. With it I can wield neither sword nor spear, and I am become a fit associate for old men, not for hardy warriors."

Miach had a stone hut, of beehive shape, which he used for his experiments, and thither Nuada accompanied him. The leech caused the former king to lie down upon a couch. He then kindled a fire of herbs which filled the room with a thick smoke and a pleasant odor, lulling the maimed man into unconsciousness. Miach took the severed hand (which had been recovered from the field of Moytura and carefully treated so that it might neither wither nor decay) and laid it against his patient's arm. In a high voice he chanted:

"Joint to joint, and sinew to sinew."

Then he left Nuada, who continued in a profound slumber.

After seventy-two hours the young leech returned to the hut, where he found, as he expected, that the hand had again grown to the stump. Miach straightway folded the arms of the unconscious man so that the once injured hand lay upon the heart. As the leech pronounced a terrible incantation, blood began to flow from the arm into the hand, but the bones were still stiff. Therefore, taking from his sporan a white powder made from the ashes of bulrushes, Miach rubbed the hand. At the end of the next seventy-two hours Nuada opened his eyes, and, quite as though he had never been mutilated, he extended his arm and grasped a sword that lay beside the couch. When he realized that he had regained all his former vigor, he embraced the leech. Later he gave the youth many costly gifts, but such was his courtesy that he said no word of reproof to Diancecht.

This miraculous cure was accomplished only two days before the gathering of the nobles to consider the state of the kingdom after the flight of Bres. With unanimous acclaim Nuada was reëlected High King of Eriu and was instantly summoned to Tara for his crowning. The Stone of Fal roared loudly as he stood upon it after he had received the diadem from the chief druid; throughout the country there was joy that the popular former king was again to direct the fortunes of the Dedannans. Since he was of different temper from Bres, who had refused to take counsel with the leaders of his people, Nuada promptly asked that at the end of six months the nobles should reassemble at Tara to lay before him plans for withstanding the Fomorians, and tell him what help each part of the island would be able to give in the approaching conflict.

When the councillors met once more, the king held a great feast; nevertheless, in spite of abundant food and drink, not a man was cheerful. The shadow of the impending invasion hung over the hall. But a champion who was to surpass all former champions was even then on the way to offer his services to Nuada.

VI

THE MARVELOUS COW

Cow of the cows of Eriu,
Give me milk for my pails.
Five hundred men must count on thee,
For as thy gift their strength shall be,
O cow that never fails!

HE host who took part in the Battle of Moytura were not the first Dedannans to settle in Eriu. Several years before this, three brothers, noblemen, having had a difference with their king, decided to leave their country in the northern isles. They sailed southward, were hospitably greeted by the Fir Bolg, and given land on the northern coast. Here they practiced the art of smiths, and attained high honor among their adopted countrymen. MacKineely, one of the brothers, became lord of the district where they lived.

Even at that time the Fomorians were raiding the Irish coast. The Fir Bolg king was energetic in repelling pirate expeditions, and none gave him greater aid, not only by skill in making and repairing weapons, but by prowess in using them, than did the three

Dedannan brothers, MacKineely, Gavida, and Mac-
Samthann.

About this time MacKineely had come into possession of a cow, the Glas, or Blue One, which gave more
milk than any other in Eriu. She had, therefore, to be
watched constantly, lest she be stolen. The Fomorians soon heard of her wonderful milk-giving, and,
hoping that they might seize her, they made the vicinity of MacKineely's dwelling the objective of many
of their raids. However, the Glas was successfully
guarded, and the Fomorians always had to withdraw
after heavy losses.

Balor, the Fomorian High King, grew more and
more angry, for he had set his heart upon adding the
miraculous animal to the royal herd, and he determined to accomplish by guile what he had been unable to achieve by force. One of his druids changed
him into a red-headed little boy, and he was secretly
landed at the edge of a sheltered bay in northern
Eriu, near a road which led from MacKineely's dun,
or fortified dwelling, to Gavida's forge. Along this
road, Balor had learned, MacKineely was soon to
pass, for his own forge was out of repair and he was
going to his brother's to make new swords. Since
he feared to leave her at home, he was to take with
him the invaluable cow.

When MacKineely reached the smithy of Gavida, he met his younger brother, MacSamthann, bound on a like errand. MacSamthann had with him a quantity of findrinny, a white bronze highly prized for sword-blades and spear-heads.

"If thou wilt take this halter, O Brother," said MacKineely, "and watch my cow, I shall take thy bronze and see to the shaping of the swords!"

Knowing that MacKineely was the cleverest smith in the family, MacSamthann promptly agreed. The cow was led to a patch of grass where she might graze, while her new keeper sat comfortably in the shade of an oak tree. He was too far from the smithy to know what went on, and there was no window facing him. He could hear only the clink of metal.

Round a corner of the building appeared a red-headed lad, who shyly approached and stood for some minutes gazing at MacSamthann. The smith returned the gaze in friendly fashion.

"That is a cow of the cows thou hast," said the boy.

MacSamthann cared more for praise of what belonged to him or to his family than for any other praise.

"Thou beholdest the finest of the cows of Eriu," he answered warmly. "No other gives so much or so rich milk as this cow of my brother's."

"Her fame is widespread. I have heard my father speak of her. Thou shouldst be watchful that she does not fall into the hands of the Fomorians."

"Often have they tried to obtain her. Their last three raids have been near the dun of my elder brother, MacKineely; but we have driven them off and kept our treasure safe. Even now my brother is hammering new swords, that we may be the better prepared to defend ourselves when the pirates come again."

"Are those thy brothers at the forge yonder?" asked the boy.

"They are," replied MacSamthann; "MacKineely, the elder, and Gavida, the younger."

"Unusual is the findrinny which MacKineely has for his own swords."

"What sayest thou?" said MacSamthann, leaning forward with interest.

"Just now I heard the younger man say to his companion, 'Why dost thou not take the white bronze for thine own swords, O MacKineely, and leave the iron for MacSamthann?' And MacKineely answered, 'I will do so!' Art thou MacSamthann?" asked the boy.

The smith was a quick-tempered man, not given to reasoning. Never before had he possessed findrinny

of so fine a quality as that he had given MacKineely.
Without distrusting a boy whom he had seen for the
first time only a few minutes earlier, who, moreover,
gave him information which agreed not at all with the
character of his brothers, he shouted, "I am!"

His face flushed scarlet with rage and he sprang to
his feet.

"That findrinny is mine! They would trick me! O
wicked men, well do they know that I cannot leave
the most valued possession of our family, and so they
plot against me!"

"For a warrior there were better work at the forge
than playing herdsman here, a task that could be
performed by any boy," answered the other, cun-
ningly taking advantage of the Dedannan's jealous
fury.

"Thou speakest truth, O Boy! Couldst thou not
hold the halter of this cow for a little? I would go and
foil these plotters. Soon shall I return and pay thee
well for thy service."

"I ask no payment," said the lad humbly.

MacSamthann threw the rope to the stranger and
went running towards the smithy. Had he paused to
look behind him, he would have seen the red-haired
gilly urging the cow into a gallop and disappearing
with her over the hill. MacSamthann, however, was

so eager to reach his brothers that he did not hear the thud of hoofs.

When he reached the door of the smithy, his anger had risen to such a height that he stood spluttering on the threshold. Gavida and MacKineely looked up from their work.

"So ye would take advantage of me, elder Brothers, and steal my findrinny?" cried MacSamthann, when he could find his voice. "But I have come to show you that I can fight for what is mine."

He put his hand to his sword and half drew it from his belt.

Gavida rushed upon him and pinioned his arms, while MacKineely cried:

"Hold, O MacSamthann! These are hard words. Naught have we done amiss. See, here is one of thy weapons completed, and one of my own. That of findrinny fits thy hand; that of iron, mine. Try them, and learn if I do not tell thee truth!"

Gavida, feeling his brother's muscles relax, loosed his hold. MacSamthann was ashamed; his anger left him quickly.

"Thy pardon, O Brothers," he said. "I have been too hasty in believing a boy's idle tales."

Suddenly he started; his face paled and he looked confused.

At that instant Gavida asked:

"Where, O MacSamthann, is the cow we entrusted to thee?"

"A good watchman art thou," sneered MacKineely.

MacSamthann hastily explained his meeting with the red-haired lad.

"This is some trick of the Fomorians!" cried MacKineely, rushing to the door, followed by the others.

They looked out; not a trace of boy or cow was to be seen. In anger and grief, MacKineely turned to his younger brother and gave him a stout box on the ear, to which MacSamthann meekly submitted.

"This is no time for further rage; anger has already lost us too much," interposed Gavida. "Let us hasten and overtake the thief, if we can."

Seizing swords and spears, the three men hurried along the road, following well-known hoof-prints in the moist earth.

But the disguised Balor could not be overtaken. He had already reached the bay where waited the boat which had brought him. Changing his shape, he became once more the Fomorian king, and directed his men carefully to embark the cow. This they did with as much speed as possible, but it was at best an undertaking requiring time, and they had not pushed

far from land when MacKineely, Gavida, and Mac-
Samthann reached the rocks. The Fomorians bent to
their oars, their sail filled, and their boat gathered
headway, as the three men on shore let fly their javelins. However, the pirates had passed out of range of
even the longest cast. They cried out jeeringly; their
leader stood up and made a derisive gesture at his desperate pursuers; but the cow, as if realizing that she
was being taken from the island of her birth, lowed
plaintively.

"It is Balor himself!" exclaimed the three brothers,
upon seeing the giant figure of the Fomorian king.
MacKineely was so distraught that he drew his sword
and flung it after the retreating ship; the blade cut
through the gleaming waters, and an ever-widening
circle rippled from the place where it sank.

For many days following the loss of the Glas, Mac-
Kineely, ordinarily one of the merriest of men, was
overcome by gloom. He thought out and abandoned
many schemes for regaining the cow: a military expedition would be out of the question because of the
high rocks, or tors, which had given Tory Island its
name; he knew of no magic that would avail. His
brothers did their utmost to cheer him, but without
success until MacSamthann suggested that Mac-
Kineely consult a woman learned in sorcery.

Is women & cows so closely connected?

"Through thee I have lost the Glas; mayhap through thee I shall regain her," answered MacKineely, brightening. "I like thine advice."

With that the eldest brother went straightway to the house of the wise woman, whom he found pounding herbs in a metal bowl. Although of a wild, forbidding appearance, she was kind at heart, and she listened sympathetically to MacKineely's account of the various stratagems which he had considered. She already knew of his loss, for the story had spread rapidly.

"Difficult is it for me to advise thee," she said. "Well thou knowest that Balor is unlike ordinary men. He has a giant's frame; one of his eyes, though usually kept closed as if he were blind, has such a deadly glance that it will slay any one within twenty-five feet. When Balor was a young boy, he was passing a house wherein druids had been stirring magic potions and had set them by a window to cool. As he paused at the window, the fumes of the deadly poisons entered his eye, so that ever since it has been more to be feared than sword or sling or javelin. Balor's eyelid closed at the same time and he is unable to raise it alone; therefore, when he goes to battle, he has beside him a youth whose duty it is to roll back the eyelid at the king's request. Ill were it for thee to

come into his presence and have him know thee; undoubtedly he keeps the cow on the green in front of
his palace, where thou wouldst run danger from the
terrible eye. Against that I have no power, but what
is possible to do for thee, that will I. Take this ring.
Place it upon the third finger of thy right hand. Turn
it twice, and thou shalt have the appearance of a
young girl; turn it twice more, and thou shalt regain
thine own shape. Guard the ring well, for, shouldst
thou lose it, thou must continue in the shape thou art
then wearing. Mayhap, if thy followers will row thee
close to Tory Island, thou canst land unseen, and,
in the guise of a young woman, win news of the
whereabouts of the cow, learning how to deliver her
from the Fomorians. Thou shalt never get her till
thou hast slain Balor."

Thanking the druidess, MacKineely hastened home
and made preparations for immediate departure.

VII

THE STORY OF ETHNE

There's a clamor of swords and voices,
A sharp command at the gate.
Is it the word of Balor the King?
Is it the call of Fate?

OT many days later, MacKineely was clambering over the rocks leading to one of the less frequented roads through the Fomorian country. He looked like a woman from a foreign land; if he should be asked questions, he was prepared to say that he came from Wales. He carried a harp, for he was a skilled musician and was said to sing as sweetly as any bard in Eriu. He thought that his music might aid him in reaching those who could give him the information he desired.

MacKineely had not traveled far when he saw in the distance a great tower commanding a wide view of the sea. As he drew near, he noticed that this tower was surrounded by a wall in which was a gate guarded by an armed man who stood in the shadow of the battlements, trying to avoid the hot sun.

"Here is one who can tell me something," thought MacKineely.

"Victory and blessing be upon thee, O Warrior," he said aloud. "Before whose fort or dwelling am I, and whither does this road lead?"

The soldier shifted his spear from one hand to the other and looked intently at MacKineely before answering. If the man had been suspicious, his doubts were set at rest, for he replied pleasantly, in a low drawl:

"Well is it that thou comest from another country, O Maiden, for it might chance to fare ill with thee wert thou of the Fomorians and at this gate, even though thou art of womankind."

"And if I were a man, what reason is there that I should not be here? Are not roads in the Fomorian country for men and women alike?"

The sentry, seeing MacKineely's annoyance that his question had not been directly answered, continued:

"Thou dost not understand, and I shall tell thee. The road along which thou journeyest goes no further; the king's command is that none may travel it save those having business at the tower. Within dwells the only child of Balor, High King of the Fomorians. She has been kept here since babyhood because, before her birth, it was prophesied that Balor should be slain by his grandson. The king thereupon swore a mighty oath that his daughter should never marry. Her companions are twelve women from the noblest families of our people. Never has Ethne seen a young man but at a distance; the work in out-houses and gardens is done by women; my fellow guards and I are the only men near at hand, and she cannot see us, for she never passes this gate. An aged druid is permitted to visit the tower to instruct Ethne and her women in religion. But graybeards are fit companions of women," he added scornfully.

"Ethne is now seventeen years old, and she is said to be the loveliest princess ever born on Tory Island. No luxury is denied her, and women skilled in all arts are brought hither for her pleasure. I see thou hast a harp. Perchance thou art one of them?"

MacKineely, not yet accustomed to his new appearance, and naturally truthful, was on the point of answering emphatically "No," when it occurred to him that, if he said he had heard of Ethne and had come to the tower hoping for a chance to entertain her, he might not only be brought into her presence, but, through her, reach the court of Balor and find the lost cow.

"If this be Ethne's dwelling, I have chosen the right road. I am a maiden from Wales, skilled in playing the harp and in singing. While in the country of the Fomorians with my brother, I was told of the lovely Ethne, and I set out to learn if I might not remain with her a few days and sing to her."

Although the man-at-arms was not quick-witted, he had an eye for comeliness, and MacKineely had been changed into a girl far from ugly.

"I doubt not that they will welcome thee, O Maiden," said the sentry admiringly.

"Tell me further of Ethne," urged MacKineely, before the Fomorian could continue. "If I am to see her, I would know more about her, lest I speak unwisely."

"I am told that of late she has been watching the fishermen in their boats. Some of them have rowed very near the shore, and Ethne, noticing that they are different from the women with her, and from the druid, has asked many questions difficult to answer. They say her sleep has been troubled, and from the descriptions she gives of those who have appeared to her in visions, she seems to be dreaming of fisher-folk. Her women are endeavoring to distract her from such dreams and queries, but, so far, with little success."

"I may succeed where they have failed."

"Thy opportunity may be soon. Yonder comes an aged sailor who every week brings fish for the princess and is met at the gate by one of her companions."

MacKineely saw a cart approaching slowly. As he looked down the road, the gate behind him opened, and a tall, dark woman stepped out. Noticing a stranger, she hesitated, with an inquiring glance at the guard, who reassured her and explained the mission of the maiden from Wales. Accepting the explanation, the woman led MacKineely within the enclosure.

"For a month past," she said, "my mistress has seemed changed. She has lost her former gayety and wanders alone on the high rocks by the sea where there is no wall. Constantly she asks us what persons are those who row by in coracles, and describes to us strong, broad-chested beings of whom she has dreamed. As we are forbidden to mention men, we explain as best we may — and the task is difficult."

By this time MacKineely and his guide had reached the entrance to Ethne's bower, set in the midst of gardens even more beautiful than those through which the visitor had already come. Within the arbor sat the princess, dressed in a white tunic; from her shoulders fell a yellow cloak; round her neck was a chain of precious stones. The splendor of her dark beauty burst upon MacKineely, so that he was for some seconds speechless.

"Whether or no Ethne suffers from the sickness of love," thought he, "I shall suffer from it henceforth."

The princess received the supposed Welsh girl graciously, though without much show of interest.

"Wilt thou not play for me, O Maiden? The music of thy country is far-famed."

MacKineely raised his harp, and with deft fingers sounded melodious chords; Ethne and her companions settled themselves to listen. He resolved that, if ever a singer put his heart into words and music, he would do so then.

He sang:

> Color of the foxglove,
>   Color of the rose,
> The minstrel sings the beauty
>   Every poet knows.
>
> Eyes of maiden wonder
>   Gleam with love's delight;
> He that knows their shining
>   Knows a starlit night.
>
> More gently than a seed falls,
>   Or berry from a tree,
> Love shall fall within the heart,
>   Blossom wondrously.

almost alone
spell

When MacKineely had finished, there was silence, disturbed only by the sound of surf on the rocks below the tower. Of the twelve ladies with the princess, only one, the youngest, her closest friend, Blanaid, was pleased with the song; the others were troubled by the mention of love, yet this was scarcely a sufficient reason for objecting to Ethne's having the stranger for a guest.

Ethne spoke:

"Well hast thou sung, O Maiden, and thy song shall have its full recompense. Wilt thou not stay with me here? For I would ask thee about many things."

Disguising his joy behind a modest demeanor, MacKineely consented to remain. As the women murmured among themselves, the lady-in-waiting who had brought him into the garden led him to the room in the tower where the princess directed that he be lodged, and, although he spoke agreeably to the attendant, she now answered him curtly.

Throughout the day, Ethne kept the Welsh girl by her side. She dismissed her other companions, save Blanaid, and at last sent her off, too. In the evening, the supposed maiden sang again, beginning with the words:

> O waves that are rushing in rapture
> Where waits, unresisting, the sand,
> Waves, destined never to capture
> The uttermost line of the land,
> Soon, the tide will be turning,
> And you will be drawn from the sand.

With this song, also, the princess was charmed. Her women were still more disturbed, but again they felt unable to object.

As for MacKineely, he was deeply in love with the princess, and thinking hard how he might reveal himself and persuade her to fly with him. During the four or five succeeding days he was more and more alone with her. The attendants muttered among themselves, till at last they ventured to complain to the princess, who silenced them with angry words:

"Never have I had a friend who would talk to me as does this maiden. She has seen much of the world, and she is willing to answer my questions and to tell me what lies beyond these walls. This ye have never done. She shall remain with me as long as she will, and take rich gifts when she goes."

Great was the consternation of Ethne's guardians. What was the Welsh woman telling? She must be dismissed at once; yet they knew Ethne was not ready to release her, and that it would be difficult, if not impossible, to deal with the stranger, who had become so devoted that she would not willingly depart from the princess. What should be done? They would consult Balor; he was their sovereign as well as the father of their charge, and he would know what ship from Wales had arrived at Tory Island, the

names of her passengers, and how soon the vessel
would return home. Reproaching themselves that
they had not sent earlier to the High King, they despatched a messenger immediately.

Fortunately for MacKineely, Blanaid told Ethne
of what had been arranged by the waiting-women, and
the princess told her new favorite. The Dedannan
realized that he was now in peril; the messenger
would return from the court bringing word that no
such woman as the Welsh girl had ever been seen by
the king or had landed on the island. He must tell
the princess the truth. As he and Ethne were walking
on the rocks in the evening, watching the wavering
pathway of the moon across the dark ocean, he con-
fessed both his identity and his love, and begged the
princess to trust herself to him. Rapidly he poured
forth his story, and, as he drew to a close, he twisted
the ring upon his right hand and stood revealed.

Her alarm upon seeing the tall, blue-eyed stranger,
with his golden hair, crimson cloak, and jeweled
sword, gradually disappeared, and under the spell of
his eager words dismay gave place to tenderness.

"O Chieftain from Eriu," she said at last, "already
must thou know what I shall say to thee. Thou hast
told me all I have learned of the world and of love. I
ask naught better than to go with thee through the

world. Thy danger is become mine, and together we must flee from this place. If all men be like thee, they will help and protect us!"

The stateliness of a princess slipped from Ethne.

Soon MacKineely said, "But now, O Ethne, we must plan to escape."

"Let us trust to Blanaid; her father is noted for his good counsel, and she is supposed to be like him. We will tell her that I am no longer Ethne of Tory Island, but Ethne of Eriu."

MacKineely reassumed his woman's disguise and returned with the princess to the tower. Ethne took Blanaid into her confidence. For a time the waiting-woman hesitated as to whether she should help her mistress to escape, but she finally yielded to Ethne's entreaties. The princess was determined; MacKineely had pointed out that once she had taken her husband's nationality she would be entitled to the protection of the men of Eriu.

After several minutes of consideration, Blanaid said:

"O Ethne, I have smoothed away the unsmoothness that lies before thee. My companions have said that thy new friend has turned thy thoughts to strange fancies. Well may we use this against them. To-morrow pretend thou imaginest that the strange

maiden is a man with whom thou hast fallen in love
— as will be easy for thee, indeed! Thy women will
think thee mad, and in this I shall encourage them.
Demand that thou be married immediately, and I
shall suggest that, to quiet thee, the druid, who
comes hither often, be summoned to perform a marriage which to thine attendants will seem mockery,
but to MacKineely and to thee will be binding."

"Thy wits, O Blanaid, are keener than the sharpest
of swords!" exclaimed Ethne in delight, kissing her
friend.

All went as Blanaid hoped. The attendants were
much disturbed by Ethne's unusual behavior, and
they easily agreed to send for the druid. Ethne and
MacKineely were married; whereupon the princess
again behaved normally, and Blanaid was heartily
congratulated by the other women for having
thought of a plan to restore Ethne's reason, and
embraced by the princess for having successfully
deceived her companions.

The more serious question of escape from the
tower now confronted the lovers. MacKineely
pointed out that, although the enclosure was carefully
guarded on the landward side, it had virtually no protection from the sea: once or twice during the day a
sentry appeared on distant rocks; at night the shore

was deserted. Evidently there was little fear that any one would attempt a landing, especially as this would be possible only during the quiet seas of summer. By water, therefore, lay the best chance of flight. The boat which had landed MacKineely was due to return, and Blanaid suggested she should meet it, go on board, and guide it to the easiest landing-place in front of the tower, where Ethne and MacKineely would be waiting.

Unfortunately, the plotters had forgotten the messenger who had been sent to Balor. The king was alarmed, and, since he could get no information of the arrival of a Welsh ship, his suspicions were aroused. He would surprise Ethne by a visit.

Ethne, MacKineely, and Blanaid made careful plans. The young waiting-woman left her mistress early upon the morning of the day when the boat of the Dedannan was due off shore; in the evening, the princess, complaining of a headache, went to her room shortly after supper. The other women followed her example, and, save for a single light shining in the window of Ethne's room, the tower was soon in darkness. The princess was quickly joined by MacKineely, who helped her in preparations for flight.

Down the stairs crept the lovers, through the silent tower, and out to the edge of the moonlit sea. Mac-

Kineely, still in his woman's guise, found difficulty in clambering over the rocks. When he reached the water, he turned the magic ring and changed his appearance to that of a Dedannan warrior. In putting out his hand to help Ethne, he felt the ring slip from his finger, and it fell noiselessly into a cranny in the rocks.

"My ring! It is lost!" he cried, wildly groping in the seaweed.

"Do not fret thyself, Belovéd. Soon thy companions will be here, and we shall be hastening towards Eriu."

They gazed seaward, but there was no sign of a boat on the shimmering ocean. Almost immediately, from the road outside the enclosure, came a sound of men's voices, followed by a challenge from the sentry.

"Who goes there?"

"Balor, High King of the Fomorians, to see his daughter!"

Hearing the soldiers, MacKineely would have transformed himself once more into a woman, but he had no time to search further for the magic ring; already Balor was inside the walls, with a man carrying a torch before him. There were cries from the women in the tower, and the Dedannan knew that Ethne's absence must have been discovered. Seeing no place for concealment, nor chance of escape over the rocks, he thrust Ethne behind him, drew his sword, adjusted his shield upon his left arm, and waited.

Balor was now calling loudly for his men-at-arms, and soon MacKineely saw the Fomorian giant approaching and, after him, men running across the grass. What MacKineely could not see was a boat suddenly shooting into the moonlight and coming up to the rocks. As he raised his shield to catch a spear hurled by Balor at close range, the boatmen leapt ashore, and, a moment later, the war cry of Eriu rang into the night air. Blanaid hurried from the boat to the side of her mistress.

The fight was short and decisive. The Fomorians hopelessly outnumbered their opponents, and soon all but two of the strangers were either killed or so badly wounded that they were unable to hold their weapons. MacKineely, in hand-to-hand conflict with Balor, slipped on a piece of seaweed, and, before the Dedannan could recover himself, the Fomorian seized him by the hair and severed his head from his body. His men managed to reach their boat, push off, and carry home to Gavida and MacSamthann the tidings of MacKineely's adventures and death.

Ethne and Blanaid were taken back to the tower.

Once out of the protection of the woman's magic, he clues

No one noticed that the waiting-woman had appeared not with the others, but from the boat; therefore Ethne's request that her favorite be allowed to remain with her was granted, although the eleven other women were dismissed by the angry king, who doubled the guard in front of the enclosure and established sentries at close intervals along the rocks. The princess was commanded to remain for a year with only the one companion, who was ordered upon pain of death not to leave her mistress. In her sorrow for MacKineely, Ethne was comforted by Blanaid. The two lived quietly in the tower, giving themselves to weaving and embroidery, and speaking often of the brief time that Ethne's husband had been with them. In due course, the princess gave birth to three baby boys, but she died when they were only three days old.

Balor's fury upon hearing of the triplets was greater than his grief for his daughter. Sending for Blanaid, he would have put her to death had not her father, a powerful chieftain, begged that she be spared. However, she was sent away from the High King's court. Ethne's children were given to an old woman, who was paid by the king to kill them. Not daring to put them to death in the daytime, she made up her mind to drown them at night in the whirlpool of an inlet near her cottage.

When MacKineely lost the magic ring, he lost also
the link binding him to the druidess in Eriu and her
power. Although no longer able to protect him, she
was well aware of all that happened to him. Her interest in the fortunes of his family continued after his
death; through her magic she knew of the birth of his
sons, and she was sure that Balor would try to kill
them. She had not power to keep them from harm;
nevertheless, it was she who inspired the old woman
to think of drowning them in the whirlpool near
the house where Blanaid had been living since her
banishment.

The crone took a boat and rowed out from shore.
Pulling in the oars, lest she go too near the swirling
waters, she let the boat drift, and held the three
children, pinned in a napkin, over the side. Unknown
to her, one of the infants slipped from the bundle and
fell into the tide, which bore him swiftly and surely
to a sandy beach, where he was deposited unconscious but unhurt. A moment later, the woman, now
near the whirlpool, released the bundle, which was
promptly caught in the dark eddy and lost forever.

Balor was overjoyed when he learned of the appar-
ent success of his wicked, unnatural plan, and he gave
an additional sum of money to the old woman. Both
were ignorant of what had really happened; not so

the druidess in Eriu, who was delighted that the waves had done what she hoped in rescuing at least one of the boys. Immediately she sent a dream wherein a shining figure appeared to Blanaid and said:

"Go to the shore of the inlet, and there on the sand below the dune find Ethne's son, who will one day be great among the men of Eriu, more famous than any other in whose veins runs the blood of the Fomorians."

Blanaid awoke and rushed to the beach, where lay the child, left by the receding tide on the warm sand. From a mark upon his chest, Blanaid recognized him, and carried him home with her. After much effort, she restored him to strength, and kept him in her charge for several months, swearing to secrecy the few servants who lived with her. Then, fearful that Balor might hear of the child and compass not only her death but his, she determined to send him secretly to his uncles in Eriu, of whom MacKineely had told Ethne in Blanaid's hearing. This she was finally able to do, through the good offices of a trader who had been urged by the druidess to visit Blanaid. Gavida and MacSamthann were overjoyed to receive the boy, and they reared him with all the care due one destined to be a valiant defender of his country.

At the time of the Dedannan invasion, the two

smiths were in a difficult position. Naturally sympathetic with the Fir Bolg because of long associa-
tion, they still retained deep pride of race. Before the
Battle of Moytura, King MacErc had wisely sent
them on a mission into the southern part of the island,
that they might not be expected to fight against men
of their own blood. After the victory of the Dedannans, both brothers were invaluable in arranging
amicable relations between their own people and the
Fir Bolg.

When King Nuada summoned his council to advise him in protecting Eriu against the threat of
Fomorian invasion, Gavida and MacSamthann were
too old to travel as far as Tara to attend the nobles'
assembly; therefore, after consulting together, they
called their nephew, now grown to manhood, before
them.

"O Lugh," said Gavida, "we have taught thee all
we know, and we have also put thee under the guidance of the best teachers. Thou art not only skilled
as a smith and as a warrior, but thou knowest the
history of thy father's people, the songs of the greatest poets — all, indeed, that is of use to a man of
imagination and of action. Now the country of thy
father is in danger from men of the very Fomorian
land in which he was slain, and it is said that the aged

but still vigorous Balor will come with the host soon to fall upon Eriu. King Nuada will ask aid of every man. Since we are too advanced in years to bear arms or to journey to the council, we would send thee, Lugh, our best gift to our country. Take this sword of thy father's, this spear that was MacSam-thann's, and this shield that was mine, and journey to the king. Victory, and the blessing of the gods be upon thee!"

Lugh, his heart beating with eagerness to serve in the Dedannan army, yet sad to leave his kindly uncles, kissed them tenderly, and thanked them for their weapons. Arming himself with these, he set out for the High King's palace.

VIII

THE NEW CHAMPION

Out from the wood at Tara, with sparkle of weapons
Help unheralded, to save the valiant from danger,
A youth advances, supple, confident, kingly;
Wondering doorkeepers murmur, and question the stranger.

UADA had not neglected to provide for the protection of Tara during the feast and the council of nobles; he had assigned two renowned warriors to act as doorkeepers of the great hall. They were to watch that no stranger appeared without his presence becoming known.

As these men stood gazing languidly towards the wood at the foot of Tara Hill, they saw a man come from among the trees and turn in the direction of the palace. The sun's rays sparkled upon his garments, which the sentinels judged to be rich enough for a great warrior, or even for a king. When he came nearer, they found their surmise had been correct; gold and silver threads were inwoven with the linen of his kilt and with the cloak which covered his shoulders. His sword-hilt was inlaid with gold; his spear had a band of gold below the barb; his shield of

all this gold- obviously related to the sun

wicker-work had a boss of shining findrinny; fair hair fell about his shoulders; fearless was the glance of his youthful eyes.

"Who goes there?" challenged one of the door-keepers.

The stranger halted, planting the butt of his spear firmly upon the ground.

"Lugh, son of a chieftain of the Dedannans," answered the young man in a pleasant voice. "I would aid the High King against the Fomorians."

"What art dost thou practice?" asked the door-keeper further.

"Question me," Lugh replied. "I am a wright."

"We need thee not," responded the older sentinel. "We have a wright already, even Luchtad, son of Luachaid."

"Question me, O Doorkeeper! I am a smith."

"We have a smith already, even Colum Cuallinech of the three new processes."

"Question me. I am a champion."

"We need thee not. We have champions: the Dagda, Ogma, and others."

"I am a harper."

"We need thee not. We have a harper already, even Abhean, son of Bicelmos, whom the men of the three gods chose."

"Question me, O Doorkeeper! I am a poet and I am an historian."

"We need thee not. Already we have a poet and historian, even En, son of Ethaman."

"I am a sorcerer also."

"We need thee not. Many are our wizards and our folk of might."

"Question me. I am a leech."

"We need thee not. We have Miach and Diancecht."

"I am a cupbearer."

"We have cupbearers already, Delt and Drucht and Daithe, Tor and Talam and Trog, Glei and Glan and Gleisi."

"Question me. I am a good brazier."

"We need thee not. We have a brazier already, even Credne Cerd."

By this time Lugh was growing discouraged. He had purposely refrained from mentioning his uncles, Gavida and MacSamthann, for he wished to be enrolled in the High King's service because of his own merits. However, he made a final attempt to please the doorkeeper.

"Go thou, O Warrior," he said, "to the king and ask if at his court there is one man who combines skill in all these arts. If so, I will turn from Tara and trouble thee no longer."

The doorkeeper, though really admiring Lugh's abilities, resolved not to make the young man aware of this impression immediately. Disappointment would test the lad's strength of character. The sentinel, therefore, when he heard the stranger's request, merely inclined his head slightly and said, "I will do that."

Once well within the house, he hastened to the throne, where Nuada was waiting in gloomy silence, for the king and his councillors had not been able to agree upon a plan of campaign against the Fomorians.

"Hail to thee, O Nuada!" cried the doorkeeper. "Help has come to us. In the lis without waits a youth who himself possesses knowledge of all the arts needed to defend Eriu: he is smith, brazier, leech, champion. Well may he be named Samildanach, Possessor of Many Arts at the Same Time. He has come to offer his service in repelling the Fomorians."

Instantly the king was alert. "I shall question and prove him. His skill may be less than thou sayest. Bring my board for fidchille."

Nuada and the other Dedannans left the hall and went to the end of the lis, or courtyard, where Lugh, in company with the remaining doorkeeper, was waiting. The young man saluted the king with becoming reverence and modesty.

"O Youth, play fidchille with me," said Nuada abruptly.

"I will indeed," responded Lugh.

King and stranger took their places at the board, and the Dedannans pressed closely about to watch the trial, for it was Nuada's custom to test in this game, which was like chess, the intelligence of any one who wished to act as his councillor. The king settled himself, assuming an attitude of indifference; Lugh sat upright with parted lips and flushed cheeks. The game progressed to a hard-fought contest; Nuada knotted his brows; this was no inexperienced stripling, but an opponent with the judgment of maturity. So absorbed in the play was the entire company that the occasional buzzing of a fly, or the breathing of spectators and players, alone disturbed the silence.

Lugh finally pursued Nuada's king over almost the entire board; at last the youth moved his castle, and, looking up with a slight smile, said, "Checkmate, O Sovereign of Eriu!"

For a moment Nuada gazed at the pieces, a trace of disappointment passing over his face. Then, with a laugh, he raised his head.

"Fairly hast thou won. Thy skill surpasseth that of all other Dedannans, for none has ever defeated me at fidchille until to-day. Indeed, thou art fit to be my councillor and my champion. Never has a man like thee entered my dun. Come straightway across the lis and into the great hall."

Amid the plaudits of the company, Lugh then revealed the name of his father, and the fact that his uncles had sent him to Tara. Upon hearing this, Nuada embraced the lad tenderly.

"No less could I have expected from such trustworthy warriors. By none couldst thou have been better taught. Welcome to this assembly; thou shalt be a rock in time of danger!"

With these words the king led the way back to the hall and to the long table at the foot of the throne. When all save Lugh were seated, there was still a vacant place at the right of the king, to which Nuada pointed.

"This seat was set aside for the wisest of my learned men, who is absent because of the infirmities of age," said the High King. "Well mayst thou sit here, for if thy skill with weapons is the equal of thy power of mind, thou art destined to be the greatest of the Dedannans."

Modestly, Lugh stood before the empty place and said:

"My thanks to thee, O King, and to thy warriors, for this greeting and for this honor. Rightly hast thou said that I have not yet proved my strength of body. Let one of thy champions now test me."

"I will be that one," said Ogma, rising.

In the middle of the hall was a huge flat-topped boulder, often used as a table, which had required seven men for its placing. Over this bent Ogma. The muscles of his arms and legs tightened as he seized the rock and, with a mighty effort, hurled it, tearing a jagged hole, through the side of the house. A murmur of astonishment went round the assembly. Lugh said nothing, but ran swiftly from the room, and soon he could be seen outside the great hole.

"Stand aside, O Men of the Dedannans, that I may restore the stone to its place!" he cried.

The warriors scattered to the corners of the room, as, through the gaping rent in the wall, the boulder, thrown with accurate aim, fell hurtling into its original position. The entire company was silent, spellbound. Then a mighty cheer acclaimed the man who had performed this marvelous feat.

After Lugh had taken the seat assigned him, one of the oldest men rose and said:

"O Nuada, let our new champion play the harp for us, that we may know if his skill in music be as great as his bodily vigor."

From the harp given him, Lugh brought forth a

haunting, slumbrous melody. Drowsiness overtook the host, and it is said that they fell asleep until the same hour on the following day, when they awoke without realizing the passage of time. Lugh played a dirge, and there was not a warrior whose face was not wet with tears nor whose voice was not choked with sobs. Swiftly, thereupon, the harper sounded a merry tune, and straightway the warriors were laughing and shouting with glee, so that they seemed a company of children.

Then Lugh laid aside the harp, and the king ordered a great feast, which lasted many hours. After that Nuada stood and addressed the assembly:

"O Dedannans, we who have seen the powers of Lugh Samildanach have faith that he will deliver us from slavery to the Fomorians. We would now have his counsel, and, that we may all show our trust in him, I would for a time yield him my throne. What say ye, O Men?"

"Thou speakest wisely, Nuada!" they cried.

Then Lugh sat upon the throne and was treated as a king, and all gave heed to his words, and he proved skillful in planning strategy for the confusion of the enemy.

At the end of thirteen days the council was dismissed, in order that each man might go to his own district to hearten his countrymen with news of the arrival of Lugh. But before the councillors separated, the learned men of all the arts, whether farmers, smiths, charioteers, leeches, judges, were directed to assemble in two weeks' time at Girley. Thither went the young warrior, taking with him the Dagda, Ogma, Gobniu the Smith, and Diancecht the Leech, that he might consult with them privately.

IX

PREPARATIONS FOR BATTLE

"Wizards, braziers, swordsmen,
Lend me of your might,
For the fate of Eriu
Hangs upon a fight."

Thus spake King Nuada,
Royal, earnest, brave.
Hearts of all who heard him
Leapt, Eriu to save.

HEN the wise men and the heroes of the Dedannans had gathered at Girley, Nuada again sat upon the throne, and at his right hand was Lugh. Then the king arose and spoke:

"Councillors and heroes, we who have captured the island of Eriu must soon show whether we have the strength to hold it. Well is it for us to remember certain things in order that we may have confidence in the justice of our cause. We have tried to make an alliance with the Fomorians, but they would not live in peace with us; instead, they laid waste the northern coast and demanded tribute, which a weak king was willing to pay them. Bres no longer

spoke the will of our people when he agreed to this demand. Now, blemished as a result of Corpre's satire,
and unfit to rule, he has fled to our enemies, and they
have made mighty preparations to take this island
and to restore him. The former king has shown that
he has a Fomorian rather than a Dedannan heart."

There was a rattle of arms, and a hoarse murmur in
approval of Nuada's words, before he continued:

"O Dedannans, we are, nevertheless, of good courage. The presence in our army of Lugh of the Many
Arts will surely give us victory; yet we must not rely
upon one man, but upon the knowledge and the skill
of each. Let Mathgen the Sorcerer, therefore, say
what he will do to aid his countrymen."

Then an aged man, wearing a black cloak orna-
mented with gold thread, fixed a piercing eye upon
Nuada, and said:

"O King, if the forthcoming battle goes against the
Dedannans, I will cause the summits of the mountains of Eriu to fall upon the Fomorians. And these
are the names of the twelve chief mountains which
will fight for us: the Slieve League, the Denna Ulad,
and the Mourne Mountains, and Slieve Bloom, and
Slieve Snechtai, Slieve Mish and Slieve Blai and
Memthenn and Slieve Maccu Belgodon, and the
Curlew Hills, and Cruachan Aigle."

"The gratitude of the Dedannans be upon thee, O Mathgen," responded the king. "Let Drucht the Cupbearer say what power he and his fellows will wield."

"Not hard to say," declared Drucht. "We will bring a mighty thirst upon the Fomorians, and they shall not find drink to quench it. Before them we will place the twelve chief lakes of Eriu, and in them the Fomorians shall find no water, in Lough Derg, Lough Luimnigh, Lough Corrib, Lough Ri, Lough Mask, Strangford Lough, Lough Laeg, Lough Neagh, Lough Foyle, Lough Gara, Lough Reagh, Marloch. Likewise, if the enemy betake themselves to the twelve chief rivers of Eriu, the Bush, Boyne, Baa, Nem, Lee, Shannon, Moy, Sligo, Erne, Finn, Liffey, Suir, these rivers will be hidden, so that there shall not be a drop of water in any of them. On the other hand, drink shall be plentiful for the Dedannans, although they remain in battle to the end of seven years."

"The thanks of thy countrymen be upon thee," said Nuada. "We have not yet heard from all the wizards of the Dedannans. Let Figol, Bechulle, and ODianann rise up before me."

Then three men of middle age advanced before the king. In their hands they held yew wands. The cloaks of two of these brothers were red; that of the other was blue. Each cloak was beautifully embroidered with circles of gold thread. Figol, the eldest of the three wizards, spoke for all.

"O Nuada!" he said, saluting the king. "If the coming battle fares ill for the Dedannans, we will enchant trees, stones, and grass that they may seem a host in arms marching against the Fomorians. We will cause three showers of fire to pour into the faces of the enemy, and we will take out of them two thirds of their valor and their bravery and their strength, so that they shall be overthrown by our might, and their heroes slain. But with every breath that the Dedannans draw, our countrymen shall have increase of strength and of bravery, and they shall not be weary even if they continue fighting for seven years."

As the wizards sat down amid the tumultuous approval of the entire company, the Dagda leaped to his feet and cried enthusiastically, "The power which ye boast, I will wield it all myself!"

A great shout of laughter greeted this assertion. The Dedannans, nevertheless, were delighted with the hero's resolve to do his best, for he was the equal of more than seven ordinary warriors.

"Thou art the Dagda, Good Hand," they cried.

"I will take the side of the men of Eriu in mutual

smiting and destruction and wizardry," he continued. "As many as hailstones under feet of herds of horses shall be the bones of the enemy under my club when we meet on the battle-field of Moytura."

When the laughter and cheering had died away, Lugh, at a sign from the king, ordered a musical branch hung with small silver bells to be shaken for silence.

"Nobly, O Men of Art," said Lugh, "have ye offered your skill to your country; but all have not yet spoken. There are some with whom I have held council already, and they have given me great cause for joy. I would have all tell their purposes. Thou, O Credne the Brazier, what wilt thou do?"

"Not hard for me to say," answered Credne. "Rivets for spears, hilts for swords, bosses and rims for shields — I will supply them all."

"And thou, O Luchtaine, what wilt thou do?"

"Whatever shields and javelin shafts shall be needed during battle, I will supply," promptly replied Luchtaine.

"Next I call upon Gobniu, smith and carpenter."

"O King and Warriors, though the men of Eriu be in battle to the end of seven years, whatever spear parts from its shaft, or sword breaks, I shall mend it forthwith. No spear-point which my hand shall forge shall make a missing cast; no skin which it pierces shall taste life thereafter. That much cannot be done by Dulb, smith of the Fomorians."

When the cheering which this statement brought forth had subsided, Lugh turned to Diancecht.

"O Diancecht, what power canst thou wield?"

"Not hard to say," answered the leech. "Not a man shall be wounded but I will make him whole for battle on the morrow, unless his head be cut off or his brains spilled or his spinal marrow severed."

"And thou, O Corpre, poet of the Dedannans, what wilt thou do?"

"I will stand upon one foot, stretch out one arm, close one eye, and recite a *glam dicinn*, a rhyme calling a curse upon the Fomorians."

"O Ogma, what wilt thou do in the battle?"

"That is not hard to say," was the answer. "I will concern myself with repelling the High King of the Fomorians and his bodyguard of twenty-seven picked men."

Soon after this, Nuada dismissed the assembly, bidding all the men in Eriu capable of bearing arms meet him in a year's time on Samain. This day, now called All Saints', was a great pagan festival. Every warrior was directed to practice meanwhile with his weapons and to see that his equipment should be in proper order for the trials of war. Nuada planned to allow the Fomorians to land without opposition, and on Samain to lead his army against them, for he hoped in this way to destroy the enemy all in one battle.

There was then in Eriu a poetess who marched with her countrymen to war, by her chants inspiring them to valorous deeds. This Amazon was called the Morrigu. She was unlike other Dedannan women, who were fair, for she had black hair, a swarthy skin, flashing black eyes, and a nose so hooked it suggested a beak. She had the power of prophecy. To consult this fierce woman went the Dagda immediately after attending the council of the king. She told him that the Fomorians would land in Connaught, and that the best place to meet them would be on the Plain of Moytura, where, some years before, the Dedannan host had won their great victory over the Fir Bolg. This augury the Dagda carried to Nuada, who felt that it would be of good omen to encounter a second enemy where he had vanquished the first.

. . . .

The gathering on the Feast of Samain was a brilliant sight. The flash of highly polished weapons set off the various colors of kilts and cloaks. Every man of the host wore new garments and carried new arms. At the head of the troops was placed a band of

Fir Bolg pipers, for the Dedannans had adopted the custom of having bagpipes played at all assemblies and upon entering battle. Since none were better players than these earlier inhabitants of Eriu, the privilege of piping was usually assigned to them. The wild music throbbed on the sharp autumn air as the warriors marched past Nuada, who stood with Lugh at his side; the soldiers brandished their spears and cheered vociferously when they came abreast of their sovereign and their champion. The numbers were carefully counted by a nobleman, appointed for the purpose, who reported to the king that the army consisted of eighteen thousand men, divided into thirds of six thousand each. At the head of two of these thirds were Ogma and the Dagda; the king himself was to lead the remaining division. It was pointed out to Lugh that his advice would be of even more value than his presence in the conflict; that if he were seriously injured he could not be replaced by any other councillor. He therefore consented to keep out of the fighting, but so half-heartedly did he yield to persuasion, that the king assigned a special tent on the hillside for the young man's occupancy and safe observation of the battle, and he appointed nine men to act as a guard and to keep the champion from rushing heedlessly into the fray.

X

THE SECOND BATTLE OF MOYTURA

The battle flows like summer tide
Across the trampled plain;
Sword-blades sing like winter wind;
Javelins flash like rain.

T the time of the hosting of the Dedannans, the Fomorians were landing on the western shores of Eriu. They were elated that no one came to meet them, for they imagined their enemies too much frightened to offer resistance.

"We shall march unopposed to the hill and the palace of Tara, with the Dedannans in hiding!" cried Balor boastfully.

Bres smiled half-heartedly; he was distrustful of the desolate countryside.

"Rejoice not too soon, O King," he answered, "for the Dedannans are brave men, skilled in the stratagems of war. Think not that we shall remain in this land without reddening our swords."

The disembarking of the Fomorians had been watched by scouts of the men of Eriu, and a messenger rode at once to the king, arriving at Girley on the night of Samain. Immediately, the Dedannan leaders were called together, and it was agreed to send the Dagda to parley with the enemy. The army would follow him to await the invaders at the Plain of Moytura, which was on the easiest route to Tara.

The champion hastened towards the Fomorians; he was quickly brought into the presence of Balor, Elotha, and Bres. The feelings with which the late king and the Dagda looked upon each other were with difficulty controlled: Bres, however, tried to appear unconcerned; he felt that he had the upper hand, for he was marching with the greatest host that had ever invaded Eriu, and the allied kings were pledged to set him again upon the throne, despite laws and possible armed resistance. The Dagda decided to be wary, for his object was to delay the impending battle as long as he could.

"O Kings of the Fomorians," he said, "well do we know of the vast army which has come to enforce tribute. Our High King has already summoned his councillors to meet him, and he has directed his warriors not to oppose your landing."

"Ye will be wise to pay promptly what is owing for the past as well as what we demand for the present," Balor replied, encouraged by the champion's confession that the Dedannan soldiers had been withdrawn from the coast at the order of Nuada.

"They are, in truth, afraid," thought the Fomorian king; adding aloud, "Never, O Champion, have so many trained men joined in one expedition as are now come from Tory Island. The fleet that brought us was a bridge of boats from our land to Eriu."

"Well is it that a messenger has been sent to tell us the tribute is being made ready, and it were ill-done should we treat a herald inhospitably," interposed Elotha, who did not like Balor's vaunting, and who remembered also the story of the indignity which Bres had put upon the Dagda.

"Thou shalt feast with us to-night," added the former king, with the evident intention of making tardy amends for his previous behavior.

In spite of the Dedannan hero's strength, and his ability with weapons, he had one weakness — the vice of gluttony; his eyes sparkled when he heard the Fomorian invitation, and he cried, "I will sup with you, indeed!"

Elotha and Bres were not inspired entirely by the desire to be gracious to the Dagda; they knew of the champion's liking for good food and drink, and they had at the back of their minds the hope that he might unfit himself to fight. Special preparations, accordingly, were made to feed the Dedannan envoy, who was of giant size — nearly as large as Balor himself.

The Fomorian king's own cauldron was brought and set upon the fire, and in this great pot was prepared a porridge of fourscore gallons of new milk, into which were thrown goats, sheep, and swine. While the broth was cooking, the Dagda took a huge ladle and began to eat.

"Never shalt thou reproach us with lack of hospitality," said Balor; adding, in a half-joking tone, "If thou dost not consume all of this, thou shalt be put to death. Eat thy fill, therefore!"

"Good food this, if its broth attain what its taste attains!" exclaimed the Dagda, helping himself greedily.

The Fomorians ate little of the mixture themselves, so amused were they in watching the Dagda, who, when he had dipped up all that he could with the ladle, tilted the cauldron as if it were a mug and drained it. He then bade good-night to those who had entertained him and started for the tent where he was to sleep.

Although he had eaten and drunk so much that his brain was clouded and he walked unsteadily, he declined offers of assistance. In the darkness, he wandered from the camp, dragging after him his huge club, which cut in the earth a furrow so deep that it was later said to be fit for the boundary ditch of a

province. At last, he came to the seashore, to a place
called the Strand of Eba, where, overcome by drowsiness, he lay down in the sand and, pulling his brown
cloak over him, he slept. He did not waken until the
afternoon of the next day, when he was much aston-
ished and mortified to find how he had strayed to the
edge of the sea. He tried to discover the Fomorian
camp, but in the early morning the invaders had
pushed forward on their march to Tara, and the
Dagda saw only trampled grass and ashes of the fires
kindled the preceding night by the now vanished
army. With difficulty, he made his way to the Plain
of Moytura and safely regained the Dedannan forces.
Of course he had little to report, and he was well up-
braided by Nuada.

In the meantime, the Fomorians, misled by the
news that the men of Eriu were in council concerning
the tribute, continued in the delusion that they would
meet with no resistance. Their army, therefore,
marched in leisurely fashion to the Plain of Moytura,
intending to pitch camp. Great was their surprise to
find awaiting them the Dedannans drawn up in line
of battle.

"True were my prophecies, O Indech," said Bres to
the son of De Domnan. "The enemy will risk a trial
of arms."

"We will grant them this, and their bones shall be broken unless they pay their tribute."

Although, upon seeing the Dedannans, the invaders were taken aback, they quickly formed for action and were exhorted by their leaders. Every chief and champion had been supplied with thick armor of leather, and a helmet of the same, reënforced with findrinny; each soldier had a new spear, sword, and shield.

The Dedannans decided to let their opponents attack; therefore, after Nuada and Lugh had briefly exhorted the army, every man steeled himself to meet the shock of onset.

When Nuada saw the Fomorians rushing upon him, shouting their battle-cry, he said to his charioteer, "Surely the meeting with the enemy will be a striking of the head against a cliff, a hand in a nest of serpents, a face close to the fire."

At that moment the Fomorians advanced within range of a spear, and the air was soon thick with flying javelins. Then the warriors drew their swords, and there was a sound of metal scraping against metal, of wood splintering, when shields or spears were hacked to pieces. Mingled with this din were the heavy breathing of struggling men and the groans of the wounded. Many Dedannans who not long before

had been as spirited as thoroughbred horses were
soon quiet in the stall of death. But the Fomorians
paid dearly for this havoc: there fell two of their number for nearly every Dedannan slain. As in almost
every battle, a few men ran away; they were, however, killed instantly by braver comrades. It is said,
therefore, that in this conflict pride and shame were
side by side. Fury rose between the opposing forces.
The whistling of swords and the noise of blows became incessant. The grass grew so slippery with blood
that men falling could not rise again, but sat opposite one another with their feet touching. If they lost
their swords, they clutched at one another's throats
with bare hands, and often beat their heads together
until one man overcame the other.

In and out of the Dedannan ranks sped the Morrigu, shouting words of encouragement and stanzas of
a war song:

> Kings arise to the battle,
>   Carrying death in their hands,
> The terrible host of Dedannans,
>   Guarding their beautiful lands.
>
> Dreadful the wrath of the warriors,
>   Deadly the bite of their swords;
> Their shields are like rocks of the headland
>   Against the Fomorian hordes.

Sweet are the waters of Eriu,
  Pleasant her hillsides and plains,
The scent of her trees and her blossoms,
  Her winds and her mists and her rains.

Would ye hold them in peace, O Dedannans?
  Smite, then, till the foemen fall back,
And the ships of the foemen are fleeing,
  Tossed home with the sea-driven wrack.

Once the fierce woman came to where Lugh was straining his eyes to watch the surging throng, or pacing up and down, irritated that he could take no part in the press.

"How fares the battle?" he cried.

"Well for the Dedannans, though it is shivering, crowded, and bloody. The river is clogged with corpses."

Behind the warriors of the Dedannan army worked Gobniu the Smith, Luchtaine the Wright, Credne the Brazier, Diancecht and Miach the Leeches. The aid which they gave their countrymen in the forefront of the fighting almost justified the boasting before the battle began. The forges of Gobniu and his assistants were kept glowing; there was heard the constant clink of metal hammering metal as twisted sword-blades and spear-heads were straightened or new ones were made. Gobniu was able to forge a sword with

three blows, such was his skill, and Luchtaine made
spear-shafts with three turns of the wood, setting them
straightway in the rings of the spears. With no less
speed Credne made the rivets to hold the spear-heads
to the shafts. As for Diancecht and Miach, who
were assisted by Armed, Miach's sister, in caring for
the wounded, they had stationed themselves by a
spring which they called Slane, or Healing, whither
they carried every one who was seriously hurt. The
patient was promptly lowered into the spring, or
splashed with water, while Diancecht and Miach
chanted powerful spells. Thus the wounded were
enabled to recover so that they could fight on the
following morning.

Nightfall brought an end to the first day of battle
without a decisive victory, although the Dedannans
had a slight advantage. The Fomorians were cha-
grined; they had hoped to win in short order, and
they now suspected that the stout resistance of the
enemy was due to an organization of skilled workmen in the rear. This, if it existed, the invaders determined to destroy, and they chose for the task Ruadan, a champion of Dedannan ancestry and therefore
distinguished by light hair and blue eyes, so that he
might easily disguise himself as a Dedannan and work
his way behind the enemy lines. He was ordered to

seek out and slay the master workmen and not to re-appear until all were killed.

When the battle was resumed on the morrow, the Fomorian spy managed to skirt the flank of the opposing forces and to make his way in the direction from which he saw the gleam of fire and heard the steady blows of hammers. He soon found Gobniu and his helpers. Throwing away his spear, Ruadan approached.

"Hail, O Smith of the Smiths! I have come to thee for aid, since my casting-spear was lost yesterday and my thrusting-spear this morning. Make for me a new spear, that I may help as I should in bringing success to our people."

Gobniu was suspicious. He did not recognize the voice or the appearance of the man who spoke to him; moreover, the stranger had not addressed him by name. Gobniu decided to be cautious, though to seem friendly.

"Make, O Crom, a spear for this warrior," said he, turning to a woman who was one of his assistants.

"I will make it," she replied, blowing up her fire and working swiftly.

"Marvelous the speed of those who help thee," continued Ruadan. "I doubt if the Fomorians have such work-people."

"We have need of quickness if we would defeat the enemy," Gobniu answered; adding, "Knowest thou the whereabouts of Lugh, our champion?"

By this question the Dedannan set a trap. The smith was well aware that Lugh was not taking part in the fighting. Before the stranger could reply, the woman handed him the finished spear.

"My thanks, O Crom," said Ruadan; then he answered Gobniu's question: "Lugh is in the van of the Dedannans and the Fomorians fall before him like leaves before a high wind."

"Here is a spy of the enemy!" shouted the smith. "To arms!"

Ruadan knew at once that his position was critical for Gobniu, dropping his hammer, reached for his sword, and the other workmen ran for their weapons. The Fomorian drew back his arm and hurled at the smith, as though it were a slender javelin, the heavy thrusting-spear just given him. It pierced the Dedannan in the shoulder, quivering there until, with a mighty tug, Gobniu wrenched it out and flung it back at Ruadan. The thick barb shattered the skull of the Fomorian as though it were the bark of a tree, and he fell lifeless. Later, the body was carried to the enemy's camp, where Ruadan's mother came to raise her voice in weeping and wailing, that is, in keening, her son. And this was said to be the first time that keening was ever heard in Ireland.

Gobniu was hurried to the spring and delivered into the hands of Diancecht, who healed him without difficulty.

In the meantime, the conflict was not going so successfully for the Dedannans as on the previous day; the invaders were fighting with furious desperation, and the defenders of Eriu suffered one particularly serious disaster. Nuada's chariot was overturned and lost a wheel, so that the king was compelled to continue the battle on foot. Moreover, the handle of his irresistible sword worked loose, and the weapon had to be sent back to Gobniu for repairs. The king, borrowing an ordinary sword, pressed forward, but, at this untoward moment, Balor managed to cut his way through the Dedannan forces until he crossed swords with Nuada. The Fomorians and the Dedannans in the vicinity stopped fighting to watch the duel between the sovereigns, which was, however, of short duration, for the untrustworthy blade of Nuada suddenly snapped near the hilt, and, before his countrymen could come to his rescue, their ruler was slain.

Lugh had seen from his point of vantage the misfortune to the king's chariot, and had determined to go to the assistance of Nuada; by a ruse he had eluded the nine men of his bodyguard: calling his charioteer, he cried, "Come with me, O Domnall. The sun is hot and I would rest." The other men paid little attention to this, for they were so absorbed in watching the battle that they crowded to the edge of the hill with their backs to the tent which Lugh and Domnall entered.

"Long, O Domnall, hast thou served me, and I shall place my whole trust in thee," said Lugh. "No longer will I stay idle here. I have made what plans I can for the battle; the issue rests now with Fate and the gods. I must take sword and spear and go myself to join the Tuatha De Dannan; yet I cannot have thee yoke my chariot, for the guard would hinder thee. Lend me thy cloak; while the warriors eagerly watch the fight, I shall escape down the side of the hill. If a guard catch a glimpse of me he will think I am thou, gone upon a message. Remain here till a shout tells thee I am with our army. Do ye all then hasten to me, for in truth I believe ye will be glad of the fray!"

"Joyfully will I aid thee, for well do I know of what help thy prowess will be," replied the charioteer.

Swiftly Lugh changed his cloak and raised the tent-flap. The nine men were still intently watching the struggle between Balor and Nuada, so that the youth ran down the hill unseen. As the eager champion drew near the Dedannan host, there burst from a thousand throats a wild cry of rage and grief for the death of the king.

A moment of panic followed the slaying of Nuada; the Fomorians, seeing signs of confusion among their enemies, were preparing for a fresh onslaught when suddenly there came a shout: "O Men of Eriu, help is at hand! Lugh of the Many Arts, champion of champions, is come, and the fury of battle is upon him!"

All eyes turned to where Lugh was racing towards his countrymen. So easily he ran that he would not have brushed dew from grass; his speed was such that no bird could have outdistanced him; his long hair and his cloak floated behind him; in his right hand he brandished a casting-spear; above the silence of the two armies who paused to look at him, rose the sound of his war-cry, "Eriu co brath! Eriu forever!"

The warriors of the Dedannans took up and repeated the shout, and their courage returned. Every man now resolved to die protecting his country rather than to live in the bondage of paying tribute.

As Lugh came within spear-cast of the Fomorians, his weapon whizzed towards them, killing five of their

best soldiers. In a flash, the youth recalled the story
of his father's death, and the remembrance kindled
the desire of revenge. Standing on one foot, whirling
his sword above his head, Lugh shouted alternately
cheering words to his friends, defiance to his foes. He
closed one eye to watch narrowly the bright blade as
it hummed through the air; he ran round the Dedannans, who greeted him with delight; he plunged
forward, cutting and slashing, irresistible. Ever he
worked his way towards the High King of the Fomorians. Balor's huge bulk rose above the foaming tur-
moil. He was, at this instant, intending to follow his
victory over Nuada with a death-dealing glance that
would destroy all his enemies, and he was roaring at
his gilly to raise the lid of the baleful eye. Lugh
hoped to get behind the Fomorian and attack him before the squire could obey, but Balor had seen the
Dedannan felling enemies like dried grass, and he
cried again to the terrified gilly, "Lift up mine eyelid, O Boy!"

Not yet near enough to reach Balor with his sword,
Lugh seized a sling from the hand of a dead man,
fitted the stone, which had rolled only a few inches
away, and hurled it. The missile caught the dreaded
eye just as it was opening, and carried it through the
king's head with the ease of a knife piercing a leaf.

Like a tree shivered by a thunderbolt, Balor toppled and fell. A groan ran along the Fomorian ranks, a cheer along the Dedannans'. The flags of the defenders of Eriu waved exultantly.

Disheartened, the invading army now began to give way, and the retreat soon changed to a rout. A few small bands had enough discipline to keep together, to escape in orderly fashion towards their ships, but most of the Fomorians threw away sword and shield in their haste to flee from their enemies, who were sweeping through the stragglers and cutting them down by the hundred. However, the pursuit was halted by the desire of the victors to collect the vast amount of booty that littered the field.

Such had been the power of Lugh's cast that, before its force was spent, the stone which slew Balor felled twenty-seven men behind him. Two of them were thrown violently against Indech, who, in the confusion of the fighting, did not realize by whom he had been assailed.

"Let my poet, Loch Half-Green, be summoned," he cried in fury.

The poet, dressed in the customary green cloak which gave him his name, hastened to the king and saluted him.

"Make known to me who flung the cast that

struck these men," commanded Indech, pointing to the lifeless warriors. "Slay him if thou canst!"

"Never shall he escape my sword!" answered Loch, hurrying away.

He soon found Lugh, and the two men fought desperately, but Loch was no match for the Dedannan. When the Fomorian saw there was no hope of winning the combat, he yielded, and asked for quarter.

"I will spare thee," said Lugh, "if thou canst tell me the number of the slain among thy people."

"As to the number of common soldiers and of the artisans who came in company with the great army — for every champion and every over-king and every high chieftain of the Fomorians came with his host to the battle — only a few of the servants of the over-kings can be reckoned; these I number as eight hundred and forty. As to the men who did not reach the heart of the battle, they cannot be counted until are numbered stars of heaven and sands of sea and flakes of snow and blades of grass under feet of herds and waves of the sea in a storm, which are the white-maned horses of the lord of the sea, the son of Lir. But I know the number of over-kings and high nobles of the Fomorians who have fallen, even eighty-five thousand four hundred and sixteen. Among them, O Chief of Chiefs, thou hast slain Balor. There was a prophecy of our druids that the High King should perish by the hand of his own grandson, but the gods have given him no heir save a daughter who died long ago, and he is slain by the blow of a stranger."

"Balor has paid with his life for that of his daughter's husband, my father!" replied Lugh.

"Then is the prophecy fulfilled! O Chieftain, never shall Eriu again be plundered by the Fomorians from now until the Day of Doom!" added Loch.

"Go in peace," was the Dedannan's answer.

Saluting his former adversary the poet quickly disappeared in the direction of the Fomorian retreat.

Though most of the royal leaders of the invading army had been slaughtered, one of them, Bres, the blemished king, was still alive. He was almost surrounded, and trying desperately to keep the Dedannans in check. With a shout of joy Lugh came up to him.

"Now, O traitor to thy kingship, thine end has come!"

"My saving would be better than my killing," said Bres, determined, if he could not preserve his life by his skill with weapons, to save it by his wits.

"What would result from that?" asked Lugh.

"The kine of Eriu should be ever in milk."

"I will set this forth to one of our wise men," said

Lugh, lowering his sword and calling for a druid, who soon joined him.

"Shall Bres be spared if he gives constant milk to the kine of Eriu?" Lugh inquired.

"Bres shall not be spared," was the answer, "for he has no power over the age of the kine nor over their offspring."

"This does not save thee," said Lugh to Bres. "Is there aught else thou canst propose?"

"There is, in truth. Thy people shall, for my saving, reap a harvest in every quarter of the year."

Lugh turned again to the druid and asked, "Shall Bres be spared because of a harvest of corn every quarter for the men of Eriu?"

Again the druid shook his head, and replied:

"We now have spring for ploughing and sowing, and the beginning of summer for the end of the strength of corn; and the beginning of autumn for the end of the ripeness of corn and for reaping; winter for its gathering. But ask Bres when the men of Eriu shall plough, when they shall sow, and when they shall reap. After making known these things, he shall be spared."

Lugh repeated what the druid had said, and Bres answered, "Tuesday their ploughing, Tuesday their casting seed into the field, Tuesday their reaping."

After that Lugh bade the former king go free.

"We would not have thee in the island of Eriu. Return to the people thou hast chosen in preference to us."

Shamed, the traitor slunk off; Lugh and his companions watched till Bres was swallowed in the gathering darkness.

By this time it was nearly nightfall, and the Dedannans were too exhausted from their days of fighting to follow the few companies of Fomorians who had escaped destruction; therefore the victors camped where they were, and their fires were soon flaming brightly.

After the death of Nuada, Lugh had been generally accepted as the leader of his countrymen, and the captains of the host reported to him. Each officer gave the number of shields, spears, swords, that had fallen into the hands of his men, and the names of the dead and wounded in his command. Among those reporting was Ogma, who had picked up a Fomorian sword with a jeweled hilt which he now offered Lugh.

"Keep the sword for thine own. Well hast thou earned a reward this day," said the champion graciously.

Thanking his leader, Ogma decided to clean the weapon before he went to sleep that night. Dropping wearily by the fire, he set about this work. Suddenly, he was amazed to hear the sword speaking with a sound like metal humming through the air:

I am the sword of Tethra, king of Fomorians.
Well was I hammered and shaped of finest findrinny;
Fire leaped and roared at my forging; I shivered and thrilled
For joy that my blade would soon be singing and cutting.

Then was I borne to a boat by the leader of warriors,
Brought to the Plain of Moytura, unsheathed in the battle.
Gayly I tore the bones and the flesh of the foemen,
Scattering life-blood from many a white-throated hero.

Victory kept not a tryst with the dark-browed Fomorians —
The sun may not always be held in dungeons of darkness —
Light and life leapt to the sunshine; the swords of Dedannans
Granted release to an unwitting dweller in shadow.

Gird me, O Chief of the noble and fair-haired Dedannans!
Well shall I serve thee, defending the island of Eriu,
Her plains and her mountains, her glens and her lakes and her
        rivers,
Till her waters be dry and the crown of her greenness be withered.

"My thanks, O Sword of Tethra," said the chieftain, when the low chant was ended; "I shall indeed keep thee forever. Thy name shall be The Defender."

At the same time, in another part of the camp, the Dagda entered Lugh's tent and was pleasantly greeted.

"I have been wondering how soon thou wouldst bring me thy word of the battle. In truth, with club and with sword thou wert a destroyer of the enemy."

"I have slain thirty champions with my own blade, and but a hundred of the men of my third have perished, yet I am greatly troubled," answered the Dagda. "My cherished harp, Four-Angled-Music, has been carried away by the Fomorians. When I returned from their camp, I had little time before the battle, and I laid the harp on the ground at what was then the rear of our army; but, in the changes of fighting, the Fomorians took the ground, and the Four-Angled-One is gone. Some of the enemy were able to retreat with not only their own weapons, but with a few of ours; undoubtedly they have my harp."

"To-morrow thou shalt seek it, and I shall go with thee," answered Lugh.

XI

THE DAGDA AND HIS HARP

Silent harp of Eriu,
When wilt thou sing again?
How should a stranger know thy songs,
The loved Dedannan strain?

HE sun was already several hours high when the Dedannan army, again drawn up in fighting formation, heard the Morrigu proclaim the victory of the previous day. She was dressed in a scarlet cloak; her long black hair, bound by a golden circlet, hung below her waist; she sang in a shrill, high voice:

Victory now, O Warriors of Eriu!
Chant we the glory and grace of the slain;
Honor the dead and honor the living,
Those who by battle have brought peace again!

Hang up the shield; place the spear in the corner;
Follow the plough in the furrow of earth;
Let the slim coracle glide down the tideway
Carrying our fishermen far on the firth.

May the mouths of our rivers with salmon be teeming;
Ducks in their hundreds drift through the air;
Kine in their multitudes graze on our pasture-lands;
Many a stag of points flee from his lair.

Peace on the earth and peace in the heavens;
Peace over Eriu smiling and green;
Peace on her shores and peace in her borders;
Peace to the servants of Eriu, Queen!

A deafening cheer rose from the army when the poetess had finished, for the Dedannans loved their country, and each man was proud that he had had a share in defending it. Then the Dagda led before the company a cow which had been given him by Bres in payment for digging the ditch about the former king's rath. This black beast from the royal herd had been the only reward the Dagda would take, at which the niggardly Bres had been delighted. The champion had made his choice upon the advice of his son, Angus, whose wisdom was now proven, for, when the cow lowed, all the cattle of Eriu answered. Some of them were in the act of being carried off by the Fomorians, but, upon hearing the voice of the Dagda's animal, the kine broke from their captors, galloped towards the western coast, and were soon quietly grazing upon the Plain of Moytura, where they were quickly recaptured by their former owners.

After the Dagda had tethered his cow, he sought Lugh. "I am ready," he said, "to go in quest of my harp."

"And I with thee," replied the Dedannan leader,

"but first let us ask Ogma to be our guide, for he knows the direction in which Bres fled."

The Dagda's brother willingly agreed to accompany his fellows, and they were soon on the track of the Fomorians. About midday the pursuers approached an open space near the edge of a wood, from which, as they advanced, they heard the sound of voices. Cautiously the three men moved forward, and soon they saw between fifty and a hundred of their enemies engaged in preparing a meal. They were seated in groups about enormous fires. Leaning against a tree behind Bres was the stolen harp. As the three companions crouched among the ferns, the Dagda whispered:

"Fortunate am I to have learned magic in the northern isles, for now I shall regain my harp."

"Three against a hundred — good odds!" said Ogma in an undertone, fingering his new sword.

"We shall be their equals," encouraged Lugh.

"We may not have to use our weapons, if the magic which I have bound into my harp avails. The wood of the frame is from a druid wand, and is accustomed to come to my hand when summoned."

Then, in a loud, clear voice, the champion sang:

Melodious Four-Angled-Music,
Harp of the wondrous airs,

He who is come for thy saving,
Death in the woodland dares.

Songs of summer and winter
Sweetly thy strings have sung,
Sleep-music, wailing, and laughter,
Songs of the old, the young.

Rise and come at my calling!
Let me unbind thine airs!
He who is come for thy saving,
Death in the woodland dares!

At the close of the first stanza, the harp stirred, and
a faint harmony swept across the strings. By the
time the Dagda reached the last line of the final
stanza, Four-Angled-Music rose into the air, as if
lifted by an unseen hand, and came steadily towards
the Dedannans. Bres and the Fomorians with him
were attracted by the sound behind them; they
turned and stood for a moment spellbound. Then
the former king tried to seize the harp, moving
towards him at about the height of his head, but
his hands slipped from the polished frame.

Gathering speed, the Four-Angled-One struck him
in the forehead with such force that he was instantly
killed. Nine men shared his fate; but the harp moved
serenely and swiftly forward until it sprang into the
outstretched hands of the Dagda, where it settled

itself so that he might play. The three Dedannans had risen to their feet, and Lugh and Ogma stood with drawn swords beside their fellow.

Recovering from the shock of surprise, the Fomorians, running for their weapons, shouted, "The Dedannans! The Dedannans! We are attacked!" and rushed to overwhelm the three champions; but, at that moment, the Dagda drew his fingers across the strings and played a wild song of weeping. The charging men paused, dropped their swords, and went into a frenzy of grief. The Dagda laughed; straightway he changed the tune to one with a tripping, strongly marked rhythm, and the foemen were instantly as mirthful as before they had been sad; they flung themselves about and danced in glee. Again the Dedannan changed the air; now the harp uttered a wistful, slumbrous melody, so that the Fomorians sank drowsily to the ground and were at once asleep.

The Dagda slung his harp over his shoulder and turned to his companions. "Now we may go undisturbed," he said. "Did I not tell you there would be no need for swords? That thief and traitor will never awaken," he added grimly; "the curse of Corpre has availed."

Lugh and Ogma nodded gravely.

The champions now made haste to the Plain of Moytura, where the army joyfully received them. After passing another night on the battle-field, Lugh led the Dedannans back to Tara, where the troops were disbanded. However, most of the men did not return to their homes immediately, but attended the assembly of nobles which unanimously elected Lugh High King and decided to have his coronation at once. For a week, therefore, many of the men of Eriu feasted at Tara, and they rejoiced exceedingly because they felt that their victory over the Fomorians would bring lasting peace. The great Stone of Destiny, the Lia Fail, roared when Lugh stood upon it; thus it recognized him as a rightful king.

The champion reigned many years, till his hair grew gray, his eyes dim. He was succeeded on the throne in turn by the Dagda, by Delbaeth, by Fiacach, by Findgill; and they were succeeded by three grandsons of the Dagda, MacCuill, MacCecht, and MacGrene, who ruled simultaneously and divided Ireland into three parts, over each of which reigned one of the brothers. In their time a new race came to Eriu, and the clashing of swords was again heard in the island.

XII

THE JOURNEY OF ITH

Over green waves the strangers seek thee,
    With straining oars and sails unfurled,
Eriu, goal of their hearts' adventure,
    Eriu, Queen of the Western World.

NEITHER nations nor individuals can live entirely to themselves. At the time when the events just narrated were taking place in Eriu, an Eastern race, named the Milesians, after Mil, one of their chieftains, had begun a series of migrations which brought them eventually to the island of Britain. Here they led busy, industrious lives, tilling the soil and fishing the neighboring seas. For some unexplained reason, they did not sail westward; perhaps they associated the place of the sunset with the land of the dead, in the way soldiers now speak of their fallen comrades as having "gone west." Whatever the cause, the Milesians did not discover the island of Eriu; nor did the Dedannans, intent upon their own affairs, learn of their new neighbors.

One of the Milesians, however, a chieftain named Ith, was more enterprising than others of his countrymen. On an evening of early spring, following a day of such extraordinarily clear atmosphere that no man remembered the like, Ith climbed to the top of a lofty tower which his father had built on the south-west coast of Britain, an observation post whence he could look over the sea to judge whether it would be smooth enough for fishermen on the morrow. As the warrior gazed intently towards the west, shading his eyes with his hand, he thought he saw in the distance the dim outline of another coast.

Turning to his brother, Breg, he said, "O Brother, is that land which I see yonder?"

Breg nodded slowly. "That may be land, or it may be the clouds of heaven. None from these shores has ever visited there."

"Then I shall be the first to do so," rejoined Ith.

Admiration gleamed in Breg's eyes. "Thou wert ever one for adventure. Remember that the west is where the sun disappears, and if, in thy youthful eagerness, thou goest thither, thou art risking death."

"Yet I am not young, after all," retorted Ith. "My son is already able to wield a sword, and my hair is tinged with gray."

"Thou wert always a wanderer," answered Breg, shrugging his shoulders.

"To-morrow I shall make ready for the journey,"

cried Ith joyfully. "Perchance I shall arrange a treaty with the dwellers in yonder country, that we may trade with them."

Ith found comparatively little difficulty in obtaining companions for his journey, since there are always men ready to undertake a brave exploit. He selected ninety of the most valiant and the most skilled of the Milesians; a small party, he thought, would not seem warlike and would be able to travel more rapidly than a great company. All chosen for the expedition went to work with a will, and in a short time they had embarked and set sail. Their kindred crowded the beach to watch the departure and to cheer the voyagers upon their way. Many, however, thought them foolhardy.

Without mishap, the adventurers came to land on the eastern shore of Eriu, where they were met by a shepherd, who was at first terrified, but who became friendly when he discovered that he and the strangers spoke the same tongue. When Ith noticed that there appeared to be few people in the vicinity, the herd explained that nearly all the inhabitants of Eriu had gone to a gathering at a place in the north, near the present city of Londonderry. This assembly had been summoned by the three High Kings, MacCuill, MacCecht, and MacGrene, because of a legal dispute in regard to property. One of the disputants had appealed to MacCuill; the other to MacCecht. MacGrene was to sit as judge and to hear the case argued by the most learned brehons, or lawyers, of the entire kingdom.

"However," the shepherd said in conclusion, "there is little likelihood of a settlement, for the arguments of each side are already well known, and feeling runs high. The case has been unsettled for over a year, and it is doubtful if it will be determined by peaceable means. Every man who went to the gathering took his weapons with him."

The Milesian chieftain drew his companions aside; after a short conversation, he turned again to the yokel. "Mayhap I could decide this case, for I am learned in law. Will it be possible for me to go to the assembly?"

"Truly, then thou hast arrived at a fortunate time," said the countryman. "Gladly the Dedannans and their sovereigns will welcome thee, and I myself will be thy guide."

It was arranged that Ith should take only nine of his men with him upon the journey northward, leaving the others to guard the boat and to explore the country near the coast. On the way, the friendly guide told Ith much about Eriu and the history of the Dedannans. He explained particularly that the present was not the equal of the generations of the past; especially were the kings, MacCuill, MacCecht, and MacGrene, men of less strength and ability than their grandfather, the Dagda, and the heroes of his day. Although the peasant spoke with caution, Ith realized that there was widespread dissatisfaction in Eriu; it seemed to him that the shepherd looked a trifle enviously at the stalwart Milesians. For his own part, the leader marveled at the fertility of the country he traveled through: the great central plain, with cattle grazing, and with cultivated fields; the forests abounding in game; the lakes and streams teeming with fish.

Eventually the Milesians reached the assembly of the men of Eriu, where the Dedannans looked upon them with curiosity, but without hostility. Word of the new arrivals was quickly brought to the sovereigns, and the strangers were called before the thrones upon which sat the three High Kings. Gladness filled the hearts of the rulers, for the dispute before the court had again reached a deadlock.

Ith explained his coming, his hope that there might be close relations between Eriu and his own country. To King MacGrene he added that he had heard of the quarrel between MacCuill and MacCecht, and that he had knowledge of law.

"Welcome art thou, and welcome are those with thee," graciously responded MacGrene. "Happy fortune has brought thee hither. Gladly do we welcome thee as judge."

MacGrene then set forth carefully the entire cause of disagreement between the two parties, and the arguments which had been used by the Dedannan brehons. While the king spoke, Ith's mind worked quickly; he foresaw that if he decided in favor of either contestant, the other might be made his lasting enemy. As a result, Ith would not succeed in his purpose of establishing friendly relations between Dedannans and Milesians. He determined, therefore, to give a judgment which might reconcile the brothers, but which should be expressed in such general terms that he could not be accused of interfering in a household quarrel. This he did, concluding:

"Do just righteousness. It is fitting for you to maintain a good brotherhood. It is right for you to have a good disposition. Good is your land; plenteous her harvest, her honey, her fish, her wheat, and her other grain; moderate are her heat and cold; all that is sufficient for you is in her. Act according to the laws of justice."

These words were received by the entire assembly with the silence of disappointment. MacGrene was

particularly confused; he had hoped to reunite Mac-
Cuill and MacCecht, and he knew that he could not
ask a new judgment from the stranger, for that would
be the height of discourtesy. Ith also realized his
mistake, yet he was fearful of causing still more harm
if he spoke further. Fortunately, MacGrene saved
the situation by saying:

"Brothers, and Men of the Dedannans, we owe our
thanks to Ith of the Milesians for his judgment. May
his words, working in our hearts, bring straight from
crooked! Ponder well this case; and I summon you
all to meet me here three months from to-day, that
we may again know the opinions of the brehons.
Now, O Chieftain, I bid thee and thy companions
feast with us in two hours' time in our royal tent,
that we may discuss the matters which concern
Milesians and Dedannans."

Saluting the kings, Ith accepted the royal invitation, and he and his followers withdrew to a tent set
apart for their use. Here he gave himself to moody
thoughts, but, after a time, his spirits revived, for he
remembered that he had not yet spoken of establishing trade between Britain and Eriu, and he hoped
that, by the time of the feast, the misfortune of the
morning would be forgotten. He felt MacGrene to
be well disposed, but he distrusted the dark looks of
MacCuill and MacCecht.

Without pleasure, the Dedannans prepared for a
night of carousing. As the supporters of the opposing
kings passed one another, there was a rattling of
swords and spears against shields. MacCuill and
MacCecht, glowering at each other, went to separate
tents, where they paced angrily up and down, enmity
smouldering in their hearts. MacGrene, on the other
hand, was of a happier disposition; he was not long
troubled by Ith's unfortunate lack of decision; he
wished sincerely to bring his countrymen more into
touch with the rest of the world, and he welcomed the
opportunity of possible trade with the Milesians.
However, the plans of the well-disposed were destined to be overthrown by one man who cherished
hatred; the power of the Dedannans was to be broken
by the scheming of a Fomorian.

For some time after the Second Battle of Moytura,
no Fomorian had visited Eriu, but, eventually, the
family of Balor having died out, his people landed
once more upon the Irish coast, where, since they had
lost their old arrogance, they were hospitably treated.
Among those who crossed the narrow stretch of water
dividing Tory Island from Eriu was a certain Brath,
a youth skilled in wizardry, exceedingly ugly, and of
an evil disposition. His grandfather had been slain
in the Battle of Moytura, and his father, swearing to

avenge the Fomorian defeat, had, on his death-bed, made his son promise to devote his life to destroying the Dedannans. With this object always in mind, Brath perfected himself in sorcery. In time, he ventured to visit Eriu. Since, in spite of his ugliness, he was a man both of intelligence and of courtesy, he made such a reputation among the Dedannans that he was eventually summoned to the court of Mac-Cuill, who made him chief magician and a close companion. But Brath never forgot his purpose in life, and he was continually hoping for the time when he might contribute to the downfall of his grandfather's enemies; accordingly, when the dispute arose between MacCuill and MacCecht, the sorcerer did all he could to prevent an agreement; he felt that through this quarrel might come his long-awaited chance for revenge.

While Ith avoided pronouncing a definite judgment at the assembly, Brath paid strict attention to the stranger's words; he thought he found in them the opportunity he was seeking, and his heart leapt. He hurried to MacCuill's tent soon after the king's angry withdrawal from the gathering. Lifting the tent-flap, the sorcerer addressed the sovereign:

"O MacCuill, may I enter? I bring thee good counsel."

Without answering, the enraged king motioned Brath to come in.

"Well do I know thy pain of heart that the stranger did not decide in thy favor," said the magician. "May his ill judgment fall back upon him! Yet ill judgment is the least evil that he brought."

"What meanest thou?"

"Didst thou not hear what he said of the fertility of this land, of its climate? It is an easy step from coveting to seeking possession. Might he not return to Britain, gather his people, and invade Eriu? May not his meaningless words cloak a design of conquest? MacGrene must not concur; the Dedannans have now been at peace many years; through the folly of one man shall they again have to defend their homes? If MacGrene welcomes the Milesians to his third of Eriu, little good will it do for thee and for MacCecht to deny them your harbors."

"Mayhap thou speakest sooth," muttered Mac-Cuill.

Brath pushed his advantage; he pictured the short-sightedness of MacGrene as working the overthrow of Eriu, and he appealed to MacCuill to save his people.

"I know it will irk thee to go against thy brother, but the Dedannans look to thee for leadership; save thy race from the foreigner, even as thy grandfather

helped save them in the past, and thy name ever will
be remembered with gratitude. This is no time for
words; weapons alone can ensure safety. Slay this
stranger, and his countrymen will not dare approach
Eriu; even should they attempt it, the Dedannans
will repulse them easily.''

"But the laws of hospitality? The stranger said he
was an ambassador with greetings from the kings of
Britain; his person is sacred,'' answered MacCuill,
wavering.

"Wilt hesitate to do a trifling wrong that much
good may come? Then shalt thou perish in the ruin
of thy people.''

MacCuill's vanity was appealed to. Above all
things, he wished to be distinguished among his
countrymen; now the affable MacGrene received the
love and homage of the Dedannans, and MacCuill
and MacCecht were accorded courtesy only. Mac-
Cuill keenly resented this. He could not resist the
opportunity to do what might not only satisfy his
private grudge, but might also win him the thanks
and admiration of his people.

"We shall rid ourselves of this troublesome Milesian,'' said the king, turning sharply and facing
Brath, who flushed with pleasure at the success of
his scheme. "Hast thou no plan?''

"Wise thy decision, O King! I have a plan, indeed. To-morrow, when Ith sets out to rejoin his ship, we shall follow him. He will pause during the heat of the day for rest and food. Thy skill with the javelin and my ointment for the barb will serve us well. To-night speak fairly to the chieftain, and he will think thou hast forgotten his failure to pronounce judgment. Trouble thyself little over what MacGrene promises, for it is no living messenger that will return to Britain."

The king clasped the sorcerer by the hand; blithely both went to the tent of MacGrene, who was delighted by the joviality and kindliness of MacCuill at the feast; only MacCecht was inclined to sullenness, for he could not understand how his brothers could forgive the stranger's earlier behavior; nevertheless, as the night progressed, even the third ruler was drawn out of his gloom. MacGrene eagerly agreed to the visitor's proposal to begin trade between Britain and Eriu, and he was heartily seconded by MacCuill. MacCecht was unenthusiastic and inclined to make objections, but his opposition was overborne by his brothers.

In the morning, Ith and his nine men started early from the place of assembly; they wished to lose no time in taking the tidings of their successful mission to their countrymen at home. The majority of the Dedannans had not forgiven Ith's evasion in giving judgment, so that few were present to see him start. No one, therefore, noticed MacCuill and Brath as they cautiously left camp and rode in the direction which the strangers had taken.

At noon, the shepherd who had been their guide brought the Milesians to a shady spot near a stream, where he suggested that they pause for food. All gladly agreed; the morning had been warm; they had traveled rapidly; they were hungry, thirsty, in need of rest. Soon they had lit fires and were busy cooking, when there came the sudden whizz of a javelin. The spear pierced Ith as he bent over a cooking-pit, and he fell grievously wounded. Mocking laughter came from among the trees not far from the edge of the stream. The remaining Milesians, with a cry of "Treachery!" rushed for their swords and drew together for defense. Two of the men bound Ith's wounds; two others ventured towards the wood in search of the assassins.

Suddenly a frightened horse galloped towards them, the rider crouching low upon the animal's neck. A Milesian hurled a spear, but the cast fell short; the horse swerved and dashed back into the forest. A second horse plunged from the thicket, his rider try-

ing desperately to remount. As the companions of
Ith sprang forward with shouts of "Vengeance!" the
struggling rider lost his balance and fell under his
horse's hoofs, where his skull was crushed. The animal was quickly captured and quieted, and the dead
man was recognized by the shepherd as the magician,
Brath.

The Milesians turned to the stricken Ith and carefully examined the spear that had been drawn from
his wound. To their dismay, they saw that it had
been poisoned. Their guide identified it as belonging
to MacCuill; clearly the king had been the sorcerer's
companion.

Sorrowfully, and vowing revenge, the Milesians
placed their unconscious chief upon a hastily con-
structed litter and continued their journey to the
coast. When the men guarding the ship heard the
end of the adventure in the north, they raised a great
keening. Although the shepherd assured them that
the murderous attack would be disavowed with hor-
ror by the Dedannans, the followers of Ith were determined to bring retribution upon a treacherous
people. They set forth in haste to reach their own
country, but, as they neared the shores of Britain,
their leader died.

XIII

THE PASSING OF THE DEDANNANS

Forever shall the Gaelic heart be stirred
By legends from beyond the times marked off
By men, for Gaelic eyes are touched with dream,
And Fairy music, blown along the years,
Sounds changeless melodies in Gaelic ears.

ITH shouts of joy, the Milesians in Britain crowded to welcome the returning travelers, but silence came over the multitude when they found that the ship bore the body of Ith. In solemn procession they accompanied the litter which carried the lifeless chieftain to the palace of their two kings, Eber Donn (the Dark) and Eremon, sons of Mil and nephews of the slain warrior.

The people waited outside as the corpse was taken into the great hall; when the story of the murder became known, a murmur rose among the assemblage.

"Lead us, O Kings, against those who slay and poison friendly visitors! War against Eriu!"

A lone voice here and there took up the cry, which grew louder and louder, until at last Eremon stood in the doorway with uplifted hand to order silence.

"Milesians," he said, when the tumult was quieted, "we share the wrath which fills your hearts, and we summon the nobles of our council, that we may decide how best to require atonement for the wrong which has been done. Disperse to your homes, and ye will soon know what is our determination!"

"Thou hast spoken well, O Eremon, and thou hast acted quickly," was the people's answer; then the gathering dwindled away.

In the council there was some difference of opinion as to the wiser course to pursue: Eremon, the younger king, urged that before undertaking the invasion of Eriu it would be best to send another embassy to the Dedannans, inquire into the responsibility for the death of Ith, and ascertain whether the whole people supported the murder; but Eber Donn argued that the Dedannans could not be trusted, and he demanded immediate invasion. In this he was supported by the son of the slaughtered chieftain (who now assumed his father's name) and by a majority of the nobles, so that Eremon finally gave way and agreed to immediate preparations for a military expedition.

The decision was received with general satisfaction, and the entire island was soon buzzing with industry; new ships were hastily built and old ones repaired; old weapons were strengthened and new forged, so that, in a comparatively short time, sixty-five vessels were ready to take a mighty host of fighting-men, with their wives and families, to Eriu. Only old men and women, young children, and others unable to bear arms, were left behind when the fleet set sail. A great shout, "We go to avenge our bad welcome!" filled the air as the kings' ship led the way to sea.

In the meantime, the Dedannan kingdoms had fared none too well. The shepherd's story, verified by the finding of Brath's body, caused general indignation which brought about the speedy trial of Mac-Cuill, but he was released when the judges were convinced that he had believed he was serving his country by slaying Ith; they realized that he had been played upon by the wily Brath. However, the trial of MacCuill did not improve the situation between Dedannans and Milesians; the men of Eriu knew that the men from Britain probably would endeavor to exact immediate vengeance for the wrong which had been committed, and there was talk of sending a mission to the neighboring island to offer an explanation and an apology; but it was finally decided that the Milesians would laugh at such a proceeding and

consider the Dedannans cowards. Without much enthusiasm, therefore, the dwellers in Eriu made ready
again to defend their country. They determined to
rely largely upon the skill of their druids, that magic
which their ancestors had brought from the northern isles. The wizards were to oppose with incantations the landing of the enemy, while the three kings
were to muster their armies at Tara. However, the
oldest of the magicians warned the sovereigns against
trusting overmuch to sorcery. "For," he said, "it is
known that the Milesians have with them one of the
most learned druids in the world, Amergin." Nevertheless, in spite of the warning, the kings said they
would keep to their original plan.

The ships wherein the Milesians had set out were
driven both by sails and by oars, and there was great
rivalry as to which should first reach Eriu. Ir, a
younger brother of the kings, and Ith, the son of the
dead chieftain, each had a ship of his own, and they
were racing. In his eagerness to win, Ir joined his
oarsmen on the rowers' benches, and gave his men
such help that they passed not only Ith's boat, but
that of Eber Donn and Eremon. The eldest brother,
a man of violent temper, was annoyed, and he cried:

"Ir before Ith to proceed
In truth is no good deed."

As luck would have it, at that moment the oar of Ir snapped in two, and he fell back upon the thwart with such violence that he broke his back, from which injury he died the following night. The Milesians, displeased by the angry words of Eber Donn, and by the misfortune which had succeeded them, said to one another:

"Since he has shown petty jealousy of his brother's reaching Eriu before him, it would be just if Eber Donn should not enjoy the island."

Soon the men from Britain drew near the Irish coast, but, by their spells, the Dedannan druids made the land invisible, and the ships turned northward, sailing past the eastern shore.

After a time, Eremon, vaguely conscious that something was wrong, said to Amergin, who was in the same ship:

"O Druid, all is not well. If we may trust those who have been there, by now we should have reached Eriu; yet we find no trace of land. I fear sorcery is being used against us."

"Thou speakest truth, O Eremon," answered the wizard. "Soon I shall learn what are the devices of the Dedannan druids."

With these words, Amergin went to the prow of the vessel, raised his wand of yew, and spoke magic

phrases, thereafter observing the clouds and counting
the number of sea-gulls about the ship. Suddenly,
brown cliffs and the green of grass appeared close by,
and a shout of "Land!" went up from the entire company.

"Ye see, O Eber Donn and Eremon, that we have
been sailing past Eriu. But I have overcome the Dedannan spells, and we may go ashore when we have
found a fitting harbor."

Sailing south again, the Milesians finally entered
the mouth of what is now the Kenmare River and
disembarked, though not without having first looked
carefully to see whether a landing would be interfered
with. There were to be seen, however, no Dedannans
save a few women and old men, and Amergin exclaimed, "They trusted to magic, and it has failed
them. May their swords help them no better!"

Although the men of Eriu had not resisted the
Milesians' arrival, scouts and druids kept the three
kings at Tara fully informed of all that was taking
place in the south. The three queens, Banba, Fodla,
and Eriu, straightway determined to meet the invaders, in the hope either to turn them back or to delay
their advance. Together they hastened southward
and then separated. Banba, accompanied by ten druids, encountered the invading army near Sliab, or
Mount Mish, in the present County Kerry.

When the advance guard of the invaders beheld the queen, they immediately sent back word to Eber and Eremon of the beauty and the royal appearance of the woman waiting in their path. The troops were halted, while the kings, attended by Amergin, hurried forward to parley with the Dedannan lady.

"What is thy name, O Queen?" asked the druid.

"Banba, wife to MacCecht, one of the three sovereigns of this island."

"What wouldst thou of the Milesians? Thou seest their kings here."

"O Kings, come no further into our country. Well must ye know that the slaying of Ith was an act of madness which the Dedannans have often wished undone. The slayer has been tried before a court of his people and his wickedness has been condemned. Visit it not upon us."

Eber Donn was unmoved by this plea. He answered curtly:

"O Queen, our course has been decided in council; until the fortune of war compels, or until there be a new council, our plans may not be changed."

"Since ye will not turn back, accept the chance of fate. I ask that, if ye be conquerors, ye bestow my name upon the island."

"We will do this, O Queen," said Amergin, speak-

ing as the druid-historian of his people. "Banba shall
be one of its names forever."

Queen Banba then withdrew, not without deep sorrow that she had failed to put an end to the invasion
and the army continued its march into the country.

After journeying for some distance, the Milesians
found Queen Fodla waiting in front of their host. To
her came the kings and Amergin.

"What is thy name, O Queen?" asked the Milesian
druid.

"Fodla, wife to MacCuill, king of Eriu," answered
the queen.

"Why delayest thou the progress of the Sons of
Mil?" gruffly interposed Eber Donn.

"O King, do not push on and cause war again in
this land. Bitterly has MacCuill regretted his folly."

"But has it been punished? Stand aside, lest our
soldiers treat thee harshly."

"Since thou wilt not grant that request, consent, at
least, that the land shall bear my name."

"We consent to this," replied Amergin promptly.
"Fodla shall be one of its names forever."

The queen inclined her head in acknowledgment of
Amergin's favor and then hurried away. Eremon and
the druid protested to Eber because of his incivility.

"They seek to snare us by soft words, to prevent

our conquest of the island. The Dedannans have grown weak," was the only answer that the elder sovereign would make.

When the Milesians entered the province of Meath, they were met by a woman whose beauty was such that the entire army halted without the word of command, and the men in the rear crowded to look at her. The two kings and Amergin hastened to parley.

"What is thy name, O Queen?" asked the druid courteously.

"Eriu, wife to MacGrene," she answered in a voice beautiful as the sound of water welling upward through a clear spring.

"What wouldst thou, that thou hast halted our host?" asked Amergin further.

"O Kings and Druid, come forward in friendship, not in war! This is a peaceful land, and its inhabitants censure ill deeds."

"Not through a woman will we have peace, but through our gods and our own power shall we gain victory!" cried Eber Donn.

Quickly the queen turned to him. "It matters naught to thee, for neither thou nor thy children shall have benefit from this island!" she said.

Eber Donn, reddening, was silent, and Eremon, after a few whispered words with Amergin, replied, "O

Queen, we will advance peacefully and have speech
with the kings of the Dedannans to decide what shall
be our future course."

The elder king started to interrupt, but the queen
continued:

"The kings of the Dedannans await you at the fair
hill of Tara."

"We shall push on thither," replied Eremon.

"O Sons of Mil, grant me one more request — that
my name may be continued upon this island?"

"Eriu shall be its chief name forever," responded
Amergin.

The queen then hastened to Tara to report her successful mission, and there was great satisfaction among
her people that the Milesians had agreed to consult
with the Dedannán kings. The men of Eriu were
drawn up on the brow of the hill; the invaders advanced to within a short distance of the waiting army
and halted. The armies raised their spears in salute
to each other, and Eber Donn and Eremon came to
meet MacCuill, MacCecht, and MacGrene.

"O Kings of the Dedannans," said Eber Donn, "ye
know the purpose of our journeying to Eriu; we seek
atonement for the death of our noble chieftain and
uncle, Ith. We demand satisfaction for the ill deed.
Yield the kingship of this island, and we shall arrange

for you to continue to dwell herein; or give battle at your peril. If neither offer pleases you, make us a proposal which we may accept."

"We welcome thy words, O King, and we shall deliberate upon them," said MacGrene.

The Dedannan sovereigns then retired to the rear of their army, and, after long consultation, they reappeared.

"O Sons of Mil, depart from Eriu until the end of nine days, for we cannot make our decision while the threat of your host is present," they declared.

"If my advice be carried out, it is battle there will be," replied Eber Donn as he turned to speak with Eremon. After a few hurried words with his brother, he added, "We will not grant your request, O Kings."

"Then we ask the judgment of your own druid upon this refusal, for he has not yet spoken, and we know that, if he give false judgment, he will at once perish from the spells of our wizards."

"Give judgment, O Amergin!" cried Eber Donn.

Solemnly the Milesian magician answered, "Let the land be left to the Dedannans until we come to take it by force."

"Whither shall we go?" inquired Eber.

"Nine waves' distance from the shore."

"If it were my counsel that were followed, there

would be a battle now," grumbled the elder king; but
he dared not oppose the decision of his chief druid, especially since Amergin had brought his countrymen
safely to land in the face of the Dedannan magic.

Rapidly the invaders marched south, boarded their
ships again, and sailed the distance of nine waves
from the coast. There was some complaint because of
this maneuver, but the Milesians had confidence in
their kings and in their great magician; they felt sure
that in the end all would turn to their advantage.

In the meantime, the Dedannans were overjoyed
by the departure of the enemy, and the druids cried,
"Trust to our powers that these strangers may never
again reach Eriu!"

Using their utmost art, the enchanters caused a
great wind to blow round the coast of the island, until
the waves of the sea rose and buffeted the ships of the
Milesians from side to side. So great was the disturb-
ance of the waters that the gravel and the grass were
stirred from the sea-bottom, and dead fish floated to
the surface. Many of the Milesians were terrified,
and the ships lost sight of one another. However, in
the prow of the royal vessel, Amergin stood unmoved by the tempest. He lifted his wand and uttered his most potent charms. Eber Donn approached
him.

"This is a druid wind," said the king.

"It is, indeed, unless it be higher than the mast," answered the wizard calmly. "Find out whether this be so."

Thereupon the king directed a youth to climb to the masthead. The young man promptly reported that all was calm in the air above the ship, that he could see the sunlight upon the hills of Eriu

"Shame to our druids," said Eber Donn, "if they cannot suppress the wind!"

"No shame shall it be," cried the magician, and he chanted:

> I invoke the land of Eriu!
>   Much-coursed be her fishful sea;
> Fertile be her fruit-strewn mountains;
>   May her woodlands fruit-strewn be.
>
> Let Tara be a kings' assembly
>   For the tribes of mighty Mil.
> Eriu be their bark forever;
>   Their safe harbor Tara Hill.
>
> Now I sing the land of Eriu;
>   Eber Finn on her hills shall stand;
> Eremon shall share the kingship
>   Eriu — I invoke the land!

Amergin had scarcely finished the first stanza of this invocation when the rushing waves began to subside; by the time he reached the close, the storm had vanished, the sun was shining, and the mist-clad hills lay near by.

"Let me land, and I will put to death with spear and sword every warrior in that island!" cried Eber Donn, drawing his sword.

Even as he spoke, the wind, which had died to a barely perceptible breeze, suddenly increased, and a huge wave broke over the ship, plunging the king into the sea, where he perished.

The Milesians had respected, though they could not love, Eber; so they were much shocked by his sudden death. For some time his companions even neglected the guidance of the ship; then they realized that a new leader should be chosen immediately to assist Eremon, for he could not be expected to carry upon his shoulders the entire burden of the expedition. Eber Finn (the Fair), Eremon's next brother, was speedily chosen and acclaimed by shouting from boat to boat.

The kings now divided their fleet, Eber Finn to land on the south and Eremon midway on the eastern coast, both to march towards each other in the hope that they might unite their forces before being required to give battle. The sovereigns felt that the power of the Dedannan sorceries had now been completely overcome, and that neither army would have difficulty in reaching the shore.

The landing was carried out as planned: Eber Finn brought his men safely ashore at their former landing-place, Kenmare; Eremon, with thirty ships, easily disembarked with his soldiers at what is to-day the estuary of the Boyne.

When Amergin, who accompanied Eremon, set his right foot upon the soil of Eriu, he celebrated his druidic power in a chant:

> I am the wind blowing over the sea;
> I am the racing wave, powerful, free;
> I am the murmur of tide on the shore;
> I am the ox which hath slain seven more;
> I am the vulture that resteth upon
> The rocks, and I am a tear of the sun;
> I am the fairest of tall growing plants;
> In bravery I am the wild boar who rants
> With anger; and I am a salmon for grace,
> Or lake-water, gentle, with unwrinkled face.
> I am the science of men and of gods;
> I am the spear-point which fights against odds;
> I am the fire of thought in the brain.
>
> Who shall enlighten assemblies of men?
> Who is there telleth the age of the moon?
> Who is there shows where the sun goes to rest?

Then, remembering the slaughter of fish caused by the magic storm, the druid made this prayer for good fishing:

May there be
A fish-filled sea,
A burst of fish
From waves' swish,
A sea-gale,
White hail,
A salmon throng,
Port song —
A burst of fish.

Eremon and Amergin found their progress to meet
Eber Finn unhindered, and the kings were able to
join forces as scouts brought word that the Dedannans were assembled at Sliab Mish. Hither the Milesians hastened with all speed, determined to settle
the question of the future control of the island.

In the meantime, the Dedannans had been greatly
disheartened to find their druids again unable to prevent the landing of the Milesians; but the magicians
had endeavored to explain their failure.

"We warned you, O Dedannans, that Amergin
was, perchance, favored by Fate, which is above all
other Powers; therefore we could not prevail against
him, though we might easily have vanquished lesser
magicians. Trust no longer to spells and magic, but
to your own strength and to your weapons. Give
battle to the enemy, and drive them hence by force."

With such words the dwellers in Eriu had been encouraged, and the three kings had marched their men to Sliab Mish as the place best adapted for a successful battle. MacCuill, MacCecht, and Mac-Grene then determined that, whatever the issue of the forthcoming conflict, their race would never leave the island, but that they would ask a treaty permitting them to remain even though vanquished. Heartening their men with this decision, the kings urged the Dedannans to fortify their position as rapidly as possible against the arrival of the enemy. With their backs to Sliab Mish, the entire army went to work, and soon they were ready for the expected attack of the Milesians, which was not long in coming; indeed, Eremon and Eber Finn could scarcely restrain their troops, once they had caught sight of their opponents.

Then occurred one of the most desperate battles ever fought; so violent was it, and such numbers were killed, that no detailed account has remained. The three kings of the Dedannans fell, and with them their three queens; MacCecht was slain by Eremon, MacCuill by Eber Finn, MacGrene by Amergin; when the sun had set, the conquest was complete, and it was arranged that both armies should have a truce for the night.

Early the next morning, the Dedannans sent word to the victors, asking permission to remain in the country, though renouncing the lordship of the island to their conquerors. The messenger explained the promise of the Dedannan druids that, through magic, the entire race would retire into the hills or under the lakes, where they would dwell, immortal, and whence they would from time to time revisit their beloved Eriu. Unless they chose to reveal themselves, they were to remain invisible to mortals.

Eremon and Eber Finn readily accepted this proposal of their late enemies, whose courage they admired; the Milesian kings felt that the Dedannans would be sufficiently humbled by loss of sovereignty. Moreover, Amergin also declared that he would no longer oppose the Dedannan sorcerers.

"O Messenger of the Dedannans," he said, "tell thy people the task given me by Fate is completed now that the Milesians are conquerors of Eriu. I shall soon have no more the power granted me for a brief space; from the time they enter the hills the druids of the Dedannans shall be stronger than I."

Swiftly the herald returned to his countrymen, and there was great rejoicing.

"In truth," they cried, "we will be friendly to the Sons of Mil forever!"

It was arranged that the conquered people should make their magic change upon the following day, in the presence of the entire host of the conquerors. Headed by their white-robed druids, the Dedannans marched into full view of the waiting company. The eldest druid chanted the history of his race, their devotion to art and to science, their achievements in war, the names of their kings and their great men, and, finally, the favor which they promised ever to accord to the Milesians. Then he raised his harp, and the sunlight reflected from the gold so dazzled the Milesians that no man was sure thereafter of what he saw. It seemed that the accompanying druids raised their harps of silver, and together all played music of such sweetness that the senses of the onlookers were dazed. During the tumult of melody, the Dedannans appeared to be dressed in green and to move rapidly. The side of Sliab Mish opened, and from within the mountain came a marvelous fragrance. Into the opening went a great company of the Dedannans, singing and laughing like happy children. In a miraculous way, the whole island became visible to the Milesians, who saw bands of Dedannans disappearing into other great mountains, and under many lakes, the waters of which closed over them. Until that time none of the Milesians had realized the full beauty of the land, but now every man said to his neighbor, "This is my country!"

When the vision passed, the new lords of Eriu found themselves once more facing Sliab Mish, bright in the sunshine of a summer morning. The host opposite them had vanished, and the green mountain looked as before. The conquerors gazed at one another; they felt as if they had been standing a long time in one place; a few even declared that they had been in one spot for three days and three nights; but no man was hungry or thirsty. Then Eremon advanced before them, raising his hand as a sign that he was about to speak.

"Conquerors of Eriu," he said, "wondrous has been our vision. Because of this we shall ever be set apart from other peoples, and our children and our children's children shall dream beautiful dreams. Never will the memory of what we have beheld entirely fade, nor will the sound of the magic music quite die away. When the Dedannan druid gave the history of his race, we learned that we have an ancestor in common with that great people, namely, Gael, whom we have long reverenced as one of the wisest and bravest of our early chieftains. Let us, therefore, in recognition of the favor which the Dedannans have promised us, and as a sign of our kinship with these new immortals, call ourselves henceforward the Gael. What say ye, my countrymen?"

"We will be the Gael!" cried the assemblage.

Soon afterwards, they marched to Tara, where Eremon was crowned their High King, while the Stone of Destiny roared beneath the first Irish sovereign of the Milesians. The stone was the only one of the four treasures, which the Dedannans had brought to Eriu from the northern isles of the world, that they left to their successors; the irresistible sword, the powerful spear, and the Dagda's cauldron they took with them into the hills.

The new High King immediately divided the island with his brother, Eber Finn, giving him the southern half, from the estuary of the river Boyne, and for many years the kings ruled jointly. Their people scattered through the land, and cultivated it, and traded with one another and with other nations. The Gael multiplied and prospered, and to this day many of the great families of Ireland trace their ancestry back to Eremon, Eber Finn, and Ir.

In appearance, the Milesians resembled those earlier descendants of the same far-away ancestor, Gael, — the Fir Bolg, that race with dark hair, dark skin, and dark eyes whom the Dedannans had found in the island and had conquered. The people now named Gael, or Gaels, frequently saw, during the years that followed, strangers seeming to come from the hills or the lakes, tall and stately beings, with light hair and blue eyes. These visitors were recognized as belonging to the Tuatha De Dannan, but, as century succeeded century, they came to be called, for their golden locks and fair skins, Fairies (Dwellers in Fairy Mounds, or Shee). Always they were dressed in green, color of new birth and immortality.

After a time, some of the Fairies left Eriu, migrating to enchanted islands which their druids had created far out in the western ocean. Here the Dedannans lived in a climate neither too hot nor too cold, where was spring everlasting, and to this earthly paradise they brought, now and again, men and women of the Gael. When these fortunate mortals returned to Eriu, they told marvelous tales of the Land of Youth, the Land of Promise, Silver Cloud Land, which were some of the names of this isled Fairyland.

However, as the years went on and the world grew more and more interested in mechanical inventions and less and less in Nature, the Fairies came infrequently to Eriu; nowadays, it is almost impossible to see a Fairy. When he does come, he usually appears without the majestic splendor of the Dedannans of the past; he has become merely a wee figure — one of the "Little People." Nevertheless, let none doubt the existence of the Dedannans nor their Fairy powers, for there is record of their visits and their favors to the Gael preserved to this day in the ancient books of Ireland.

And now, according to Gaelic custom, let the Place, Time, Author, and Cause of Writing of this book be chronicled. The Place is Boston, Massachusetts; the Time is the year of our Lord one thousand nine hundred and twenty-one; the Author is Norreys Jephson O'Conor, Master of Arts, and the Cause of Writing is to persuade Americans to consider the spiritual, rather than the political, history of Ireland as interpreted in the legends of the Old Irish People.

THE END

PRONOUNCING GLOSSARY

PRONOUNCING GLOSSARY

As this book is based chiefly upon early Irish sources, the pronunciation adopted by scholars of early Irish is used in nearly all instances.

Abhean: Ah'-van [1]

Amergin: Ah-vair'-gin, with *g* as in *good*

Angus Og: An'-gus Og, with *o* as in *oh*.

Armed: Ar'-medh

Balor: Bäa'-lor

Bechulle: Beh'-koo-leh

Bicelmos: Bick'-el-moss

Blai: Bly

Blanaid: Bläa'-nidh

Brath: *a* as in *wrath*

Bres: Bres

Colum Cuallinech: Col'-luv Qual'-lin-nech, with *ch* as in the Scotch *loch*

Corpre: Cor'-preh

Corrib: Cor'-riv

Credne Cerd: Cred'-neh Caird

Cridenbel: Cri'-dhen-bel

Crom: Crom, with *o* as in *on*

Cruachan Aigle: Croo'-ah-kan Eye'-gleh

Daithe: Dye'-theh, with *th* as in *thin*

Dana: Dah'-nah

De Domnan: Day Dov'-nan, with *o* as in *on*

Delbaeth: Del'-bith, with *i* as in *with*

Denna Ulad: Den'-nah Oo'-ladh

Derg: Dairg

Diancecht: Dee'-an-kecht, with *ch* as in *loch*

Domnall: Dov'-nall, with *o* as in *on*

Drucht: Droocht, with *ch* as in *loch* and *u* like *oo* in *wool*

Dulb: Doolv, with *u* like *oo* in *wool*

Dun: Doon

Eba: Eh'-vah

Eber: Eh'-ver

Elotha: Eh-loth'-ah

Eremon: Eh'-re-von

Eri: Eh'-ree

Eriu: Eh'-ree-oo, with *u* like *oo* in *too*

Ethaman: Eth'-ah-van

Ethne: Eth'-neh

Falias: Fal'-ee-ass, with the first *a* as in *mat*

Fiachach: Fee'-ach-ach

fidchille: fid-kil'-le, with *e* as in *then*

Figol: Fi'-gol, with *i* as in *is*

Findgill: Fin'-gill

Findias: Fin'-dee-ass

Findrinny: Fin'-drinny, with *y* as in *quickly*

Fir Bolg: Fear Bolg, with *o* as in *odd*

Fodla: with *o* as in *odd*

Fomorians: Foh-moh'-ree-ans

Garah: Gah'-rah

Gavida: Ga'-vidh-ah

Glas: Glass

Glei: Glay

Gleisi: Glay'-shee

Gobniu: Gob'-nee-oo

Gorias: Go'-ree-ass

Indech: In'-dech

Ir: Ear

Ith: *th* as in *thin; i* as in *it.*

Laeg: Laa'-egg

Lia Fail: Lee'-ah File

Lir: Leer

lis: liss

Lough: loch

Luachaid: Loo'-ach-idh, with *i* as in *pith*

Luchtad: Luch'-tadh, with *a* as in *wrath*

Luchtaine: Looch'-tay-neh

Lugh: Loo

Luimnigh: Looim'-nee

Maccu Belgodon: Mac'-coo Bel'-go-don

MacCecht: *ch* as in *loch*

MacCuill: Mac Queel'.

MacErc: Mac Erk'.

MacGrene: Mac Grain'-eh

MacSamthann: MacSav'-thann, with *th* as in *thin*

Mag Rein: Mag Rane

Mathgen: Math' as in *mathematics; g* as in *good*

Memthenn: Mev'-thenn, with *th* as in *thin*

Miach: Mee'-ach

Mil: *i* as in *ill*

Milesians: My-lee'-sians

Morrigu: Mor'-ree-goo

Moytura: Moy-too'-rah

Murias: Moo'-ree-ass

Neagh: Nay

Nem: Nev

Net: Ned

Nuada: Noo'-ah-tha, with *a* as in *act*

ODiannan: Oh-Dee'-an-an

Ogma: *o* as in *fog*

Reagh: Ray

Ri: Ree

Ruadan: Roo'-adh-an

Samain: Sa'-vin, with *a* as in *add*

Samildanach: Sa'-vil-da'-nach

Sliab: Slee'-av

Slieve: Slee'-vee

Snechtai: Shneck'-tee

Sreng: Shreng

Suir: Soo'-ir

Talam: Tal'-av, with the first syllable as in *talent*

Tara: Tah'-rah

Tethra: Teth'-rah

Trog: *o* as in *oh*